# Six Miles from Charleston, Five Minutes to Hell

## The Battle of Secessionville, June 16, 1862

by James A. Morgan

EMERGING CIVIL WAR SERIES

*Chris Mackowski, series editor*
*Kristopher D. White, chief historian*

# The Emerging Civil War Series

**offers compelling, easy-to-read overviews of some of the Civil War's most important battles and stories.**

*Recipient of the Army Historical Foundation's Lieutenant General Richard G. Trefry Award for contributions to the literature on the history of the U.S. Army*

**Also part of the Emerging Civil War Series:**

**Also by Jim Morgan**

# Six Miles from Charleston, Five Minutes to Hell

## The Battle of Secessionville, June 16, 1862

by James A. Morgan

EMERGING CIVIL WAR SERIES

SB
Savas Beatie
California

First edition, first printing

ISBN-13: 978-1-61121-601-1

Library of Congress Cataloging-in-Publication Data

Names: Morgan, James A., III, author.
Title: Six miles from Charleston, five minutes to hell : the Battle of Secessionville, June 16, 1862 / by Jim Morgan.
Description: El Dorado Hills, CA : Savas Beatie, [2022] | Series: Emerging civil war series | Includes bibliographical references and index. | Summary: "On June 16, 1862, Union forces tried to capture Charleston, South Carolina, by landing on one of the coastal barrier islands and marching overland to approach the city from behind. Confederates blocked the move, thus foiling the Federal army's most serious attempt to capture the city by land during the war. Federals would instead rely on a naval blockade to try, unsuccessfully, to seal off one of the most symbolically important cities of the Confederacy"-- Provided by publisher.
Identifiers: LCCN 2021055964 | ISBN 9781611216011 (paperback) | ISBN 9781611216028 (ebook)
Subjects: LCSH: Secessionville, Battle of, Secessionville, S.C., 1862.
Classification: LCC E473.92 .M67 2022 | DDC 975.7/91--dc23/eng/20211117 LC record available at https://lccn.loc.gov/2021055964

Published by
Savas Beatie LLC
989 Governor Drive, Suite 102
El Dorado Hills, California 95762
Phone: 916-941-6896
sales@savasbeatie.com
www.savasbeatie.com

Savas Beatie titles are available at special discounts for bulk purchases in the United States by corporations, institutions, and other organizations. For more details, please contact Special Sales, P.O. Box 4527, El Dorado Hills, CA 95762, or you may e-mail us at sales@savasbeatie.com, or visit our website at www.savasbeatie.com for additional information.

*I dedicate this book with love to my grandson, Elijah James Kranias, born in Aldie, Virginia, on March 18, 2020, and my granddaughter, Aria Allyn Kranias, born in Leesburg, Virginia, on July 19, 2021, in the hope that they will grow up loving and appreciating the grand story that is American history.*

# Table of Contents

# List of Maps

*Maps by Edward Alexander*

# Acknowledgments

As with any book, this one is the result of the contributions of many people. I am grateful to them all and can only hope that the final product proves to be worth their effort and meets with their approval.

My thanks go, first of all, to my friend and ECW Editor-in-Chief Chris Mackowski, who asked me to write this book. Also to Chris Kolakowski and Sarah Kay Bierle of ECW for their crackerjack editorial skills.

To Tonia "Teej" Smith of Pinehurst, NC for her long-time friendship and extensive research assistance. Teej is the best natural researcher I have ever known.

To my dear friend and brother, Jim Bloomer, and his wonderful wife, Sandy, for proofreading and many useful suggestions.

To fellow Fort Sumter CWRT board member Rick Hatcher for a memorable battlefield tromp around the Secessionville-related sites on May 9, 2020, and for generously allowing me access to his photographic collection. To another FSCWRT board member and Citadel history professor, Kyle Sinisi, for writing the Foreword. And to a third FSCWRT board member, Ed Forte, for reading the text and allowing me access to his impressive library.

To Russell Horres, Charleston historian, for detailed information on Fort Ripley.

To Doug Bostick, Charleston historian and Executive Director of the South Carolina Battleground Preservation Trust, for his patience with me as I asked numerous questions, and especially for allowing the use of the Trust's Battle of Secessionville Study Area map as a base reference.

To Secessionville historian Patrick Brennan for sending me the account of Capt. Dewitt Clinton Lewis of the 97th Pennsylvania and for graciously and patiently responding to my many questions.

To Charleston historian, Mark R. Jones, likewise for his quick and pertinent responses to my questions.

To Mary Lou Brewton, Beaufort historian, and Grace Cordial of the Beaufort Public Library for their detailed email responses to several queries.

To Mary Ann Cawley, Malcolm Hale, and Sarah Hisnanick-Murphy at the Charleston Public Library's South Carolina Room for jumping in to guide me through that wonderful collection. And to the library's Jennifer Lively and Sarah Milner for their valuable technical assistance with photographs.

To Messrs. David Swee and Charlie O'Brien, James Island landowners, who let me trespass across their properties to take photos of the 3rd New Hampshire's position across the marsh on the right flank of the Tower Battery.

Sincere thanks to you all.

PHOTO CREDITS: **Patrick Brennan (pb); P.C. Coker, III (pcc); Confederate Museum Charleston (cmc); Duke University (du); Library of Congress (loc); Chris Mackowski (cm); Maine State Archives (msa); James Morgan (jm); National Park Service (nps); Naval History and Heritage Command (nhh); New York Public Library Digital Collections (nypl); Leon Reed (lr); South Caroliniana Library, Univ. of South Carolina (scl); Tennessee State Library and Archives (tsl)**

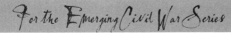

For the Emerging Civil War Series

Theodore P. Savas, *publisher*
Chris Mackowski, *series editor and co-founder*
Kristopher D. White, *chief historian and co-founder*          Maps by Edward Alexander
Sarah Keeney, *editorial consultant*                               Design and layout by Veronica Kane

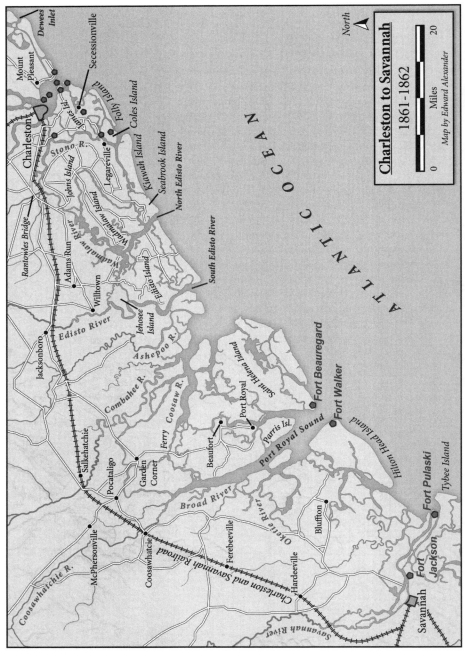

**Charleston to Savannah**—Coastal Georgia and South Carolina showing the critical Charleston and Savannah railroad as well as important campaign-related waterways, islands, and towns.

## A Brief Note About Punctuation

Names of individuals and places associated with the story of the battle of Secessionville commonly are mispronounced by those not familiar with the standard South Carolina Low Country usages. For accuracy and the reader's general knowledge, here are a few of the terms found herein that most often are mispronounced.

- Beaufort, South Carolina is pronounced "BYOO-fert." It should not be confused with the North Carolina town also named Beaufort but pronounced "BOH-fert."

- Edisto Island, the jumping off point for the Federal assault, is pronounced "ED-is-to."

- The commanding officer of the 1st South Carolina battalion was Lt. Col. Peter Gaillard, pronounced "GAY-yard."

- The commanding officer of the 1st South Carolina regiment was Col. Johnson Hagood, pronounced "HAY-good."

- The surname of Brig. Gen. States Rights Gist is pronounced with a hard "G."

- The prominent Charleston family name, Huger, is pronounced "YU-jee," a local derivation of the original French "Hyu-ZHAY."

- Another locally prominent family name, LeGare, as in Sol Legare Island where some of the preliminary fighting occurred, is pronounced "Le-GREE."

- Manigault, family name of the area's First District Commander, Col. Arthur M. Manigault, is pronounced "MAN-i-go."

- The railroad station town, Pocotaligo, is pronounced "Po-co-TALLY-go."

- The river names, Coosawhatchie, Tulifinny, and *Combahee* are pronounced "Coo-sa-HATCH-ie," "Tul-la-FINNY," and "CUM-bee" respectively.

- The town and river called Oketie (there are several alternate spellings) is pronounced "OH-ka-tee."

# Foreword

## BY DR. KYLE S. SINISI

What makes a battle important? Is it the size of the armies or the number of casualties? Or, perhaps, is it the strategic outcome of the battle itself? Although large-scale battles will always attract attention, historians have frequently shown that smaller engagements have their importance. The Civil War, especially, demonstrates this point. With over 70,000 books written on the war, there has always been room for the study of smaller battles that can inform and remind readers of lessons to be learned. Such is the case with the Battle of Secessionville on June 16, 1862.

Secessionville represents the first Union attempt to retake Charleston, SC. In a plan that germinated quickly and without any concrete strategic direction from higher headquarters, Secessionville was an accident of history. In the spring of 1862, Union strategic priorities lay elsewhere. Attempts to seize New Orleans, LA; Corinth, MS; and Richmond, VA; preoccupied the attention of Union and Confederate command authorities. Many people believed the Union capture of Richmond, especially, could spell the end of the war. Both sides thus diverted troops and all manner of material support to the struggle in Virginia. For the Union, Major General David Hunter took command of the Department of the South in April with little guidance as to how he should use his approximately 13,000 troops. Outside the possibility of conducting raids upon the Charleston and Savannah Railroad, Hunter seemed destined to do nothing of any significance as spring turned to summer in 1862. However, Hunter and his command

**Federal attempts to capture Charleston create a tangled tale.** (cm)

were about to become an exemplar of the concept of contingency in history when a slave named Robert Smalls commandeered his master's boat, the Planter, and sailed out of Charleston harbor headed for the Union blockading fleet. The randomness of Smalls's daring action changed the course of events as he brought Hunter fresh intelligence about the weakened state of Charleston's defenses. Confederate forces in the area had been drained of troops for the battles around Richmond, and a key fortification at the mouth of the Stono River had been abandoned. Although the harbor entrance to Charleston remained heavily fortified, the backdoor to the city was open.

At this point, Hunter devolved the planning of the campaign to Brigadier General Henry Benham, his second-in-command. Benham was a highly competent engineer but a dreadful commander of infantry. He possessed none of the military or social graces that would endear him to his peers or subordinates. He was, in other words, reviled. Nevertheless, Benham generated a reasonable plan to take Charleston. He wanted to land an army of two divisions on Battery Island on the Stono and then cross over to James Island. The army would then strike north to take Fort Johnson. As many believed Fort Johnson was the key to Charleston's inner harbor defenses, the fall of the fort would spell the ultimate surrender of the city. Unfortunately for the Union, neither Hunter nor Benham ever completely executed the plan. In a story reminiscent of the American army at Anzio in World War II, Hunter's invasion force landed like a beached whale on Battery Island on June 2. It then made no forward movement for two weeks. When it did finally move, Hunter had absented himself from the army, leaving Benham in command with the strangest of orders "not to advance on Charleston or attack Fort Johnson." Benham obeyed the letter of his orders, but chose instead to attack another fortification, the Tower Battery. This Confederate outpost stood on the right flank of any Union assault across James Island directed toward Fort Johnson. The Tower Battery thus stood as an obstacle to any attempt to take Johnson.

For this reason, and the battery's seemingly incessant harassing fire directed toward the Union's camps and outposts, Benham determined to attack in the early morning hours of June 16. Benham gave little time to plan the assault and even less for its preparation and execution. The attack was a disaster.

Nearly 700 Yankees were killed or wounded in what was the largest and most deadly battle fought in South Carolina during the war. Confederate losses did not exceed 200 men.

As James Morgan notes, this small battle was a decisive defeat of Union forces. Strategically, it marked the end of Union aspirations to take Charleston in 1862. The port of Charleston, and all that it could

**A monument at the Fort Lamar Heritage Preserve tells the story of the battle, including lists of the Confederate and Federal units engaged.** (cm)

provide the Confederacy, would be secure for at least another year. However, the historical significance of what became known as the Battle of Secessionville went far beyond any question of strategy. Instead, what Morgan's narrative reveals are timeless issues in the conduct of war. Many of these issues involved leadership. For the Union, David Hunter was an absentee commander who exercised no demonstrable operational control over his army. Henry Benham may have filled the leadership void, but he did it poorly with slipshod planning, preparation, and communication. Particularly troublesome was a lack of preparation in scouting the terrain. Despite having been in the area for two weeks and possessing a hot air balloon, the Union army had no one who realized that a creek and tidal marsh north of the Tower Battery would prevent any support of the main attack.

For the Confederacy, problems in the high command had the potential to be just as disabling. The defenders used a department and district organization that required far too many generals in geographical commands. Responsibilities became confused, which was made worse as a parade of officers shuffled through the commands before and during the campaign itself. Ultimately, Confederate success came to depend upon leadership at the field-grade level. Colonel Thomas Lamar commanded the Tower Battery. A planter and lawyer with no military experience, Lamar was aggressive, indefatigable, and led by example. Once Union forces landed on Battery Island, Lamar understood that an attack was possible, and he worked tirelessly to prepare his fortification. When the assault finally came in the early morning hours of June 16, Lamar was in a gun position, ready to lead the defense. Other Confederate commanders, including Alexander Smith, Peter Gaillard, and Ellison Capers, were no less ready to lead by example. Perhaps no less important, each of these men led units of South Carolinians, who were motivated by an ageless desire to defend their homeland from invasion. In the entirety of the campaign, Lamar and Gilliard would make battlefield appeals to their men that invoked the honor, prestige, and rights of their homeland.

Morgan's book is a reminder that battles, no matter how small, have the potential to reveal much about the history and the conduct of warfare. With a careful eye for the revealing anecdote and the use of

some new primary and secondary research materials, Morgan has pumped new life into the story of a little battle with great meaning.

**The Fort Lamar Heritage Preserve is managed by the South Carolina Department of Natural Resources.** (cm)

**DR. KYLE S. SINISI** *is a professor of history at the Citadel in Charleston, South Carolina.*

"Near the battery was found a painted board, with the following significant inscription: Six miles from Charleston, 16 June 1862. Five minutes to _____."

— *Philadelphia Inquirer*, July 16, 1862

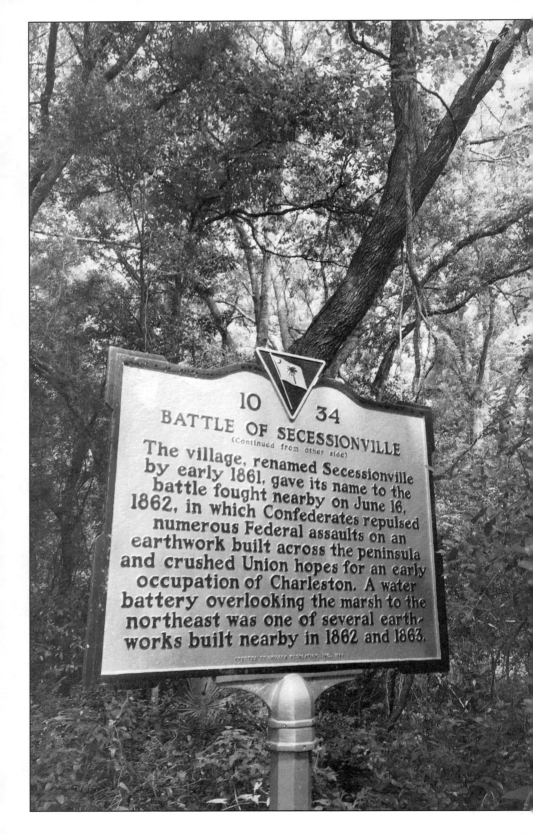

## BATTLE OF SECESSIONVILLE
(Continued from other side)

The village, renamed Secessionville by early 1861, gave its name to the battle fought nearby on June 16, 1862, in which Confederates repulsed numerous Federal assaults on an earthwork built across the peninsula and crushed Union hopes for an early occupation of Charleston. A water battery overlooking the marsh to the northeast was one of several earth-works built nearby in 1862 and 1863.

10    34

ERECTED BY CHICORA FOUNDATION, INC., 1988

# Prologue

Secessionville. Late in the momentous presidential election year of 1860, that surely would have been the perfect nickname for Charleston, South Carolina. Not knowing differently, one might reasonably believe that the name actually did refer to Charleston, which was, after all, the "Cradle of Secession." In fact, however, Secessionville was a separate place, an inconsequential village—just a handful of dwellings and other buildings located across the Ashley River on James Island and only some six miles from downtown Charleston.

Now, it is just one of more than two dozen quiet residential neighborhoods which cover the central portion of suburban James Island. It is marked primarily by the Fort Lamar Heritage Preserve, a 14-acre park on land owned by the South Carolina Department of Natural Resources and containing the partially preserved remains of the Confederate earthworks, which were the focal point of the Battle of Secessionville on June 16, 1862.

Curiously perhaps, even with so much development, an observer can still clearly see how the Secessionville peninsula becomes a narrow neck on which the Tower Battery, had an admirable position to cover the ground across which any attacking force would have to advance. (Tower Battery was later named Fort Lamar by the Confederates after its commanding officer during the fight.) At the time, the peninsula consisted largely of fallow cotton fields and ultimately narrowed to a mere 130 yards wide as the battery's construction point. This created a Thermopylae-like

A South Carolina historical marker one-half mile past Ft. Lamar notes battle information. (cm)

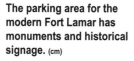

The opposite side of the same historical marker notes the original name of Secessionville: Riversville. (cm)

defile, though flanked by thick, gooey "pluff mud" marshes instead of mountains, which would become a perfect killing field.

It would be logical to assume that its fire-eating residents renamed the village, originally known as Riversville, to honor the action taken by their state on December 20, 1860. But that may not be the case.

According to a South Carolina state roadside marker not far from the remains of the earthwork, Secessionville was "an antebellum village on 14 acres, with seven lots on Savannah (later Secessionville) Creek." A local citizen, Constant H. Rivers, established it in 1851, apparently feeling that "the sandy soils and marsh breezes of James Island would protect inhabitants from the 'malarious gasses' common to the coast during the summer months." He built a home there and thus established the town.

Just when the village was renamed, who renamed it, and exactly why are matters of considerable historical conjecture. There seems to be no documentation which

The parking area for the modern Fort Lamar has monuments and historical signage. (cm)

**John C. Calhoun, vice-president under Andrew Jackson, became Jackson's bitter political enemy and the "Father of Secession." Calhoun was the primary supporter of the establishment of a Southern Confederacy.**
(loc)

would prove one view over another. Patrick Brennan, author of the 1996 battle study, Secessionville: Assault on Charleston, correctly states that the name change is "shrouded in legend." One story is that several young landowners, Rivers among them, "seceded" from their elders for unspecified reasons and organized their own community for use in the summer. There are variations on this theme, but they all beg the question of why anyone would have used the very specific political term "secession" to describe what was, essentially, just a real estate development. Moreover, when children inevitably leave home, they do not usually say that they are seceding from their parents. Clearly, there is more to the story than that.

A possible answer to the mystery lies in the timing. It all happened shortly after the failed Nashville Convention of June 1850, a gathering of most of the southern states where the idea of secession from the Union was discussed.

Organized primarily at the urging of South Carolina's John C. Calhoun, who died before the convention met, the convention's purpose focused on formulating a joint response by the southern states in the event that Congress declined to allow slavery in

**John C. Calhoun's grave is in Charleston, in St. Philip's churchyard.** (loc)

the new territories acquired as a result of the Mexican War. Delegates from all the later Confederate States except North Carolina and Louisiana attended. South Carolina and Mississippi were the two firebrands. They pushed the hardest not just for possible secession, but for immediate secession. However, they did not have broad southern support for such a radical move and were outvoted by the more moderate states. This resulted in southern acquiescence to the Compromise of 1850.

The air was hot with talk of secession in South Carolina, however. The state not only had enthusiastically supported the idea in principle longer than any other state, but even had been preparing for both the act of secession and the war that leading South Carolinians believed would follow. The state legislature passed the "Defense Act of 1850," by which it appropriated $300,000 to purchase enough arms and materiel to supply a proposed state militia of 15,000 men (larger than the U.S. Army at the time).

Considering how highly exercised almost all South Carolinians were about this, it is not unreasonable to speculate that the town's new name came out of that period of intense political turmoil. Under those circumstances, one can easily imagine the younger people joking about "seceding" from their elders.

Still, nothing about this is certain. While some references indicate, or at least imply, that the name "Secessionville" was in use early in the 1850s, others hold that it resulted from the events of 1860. Either way, "Secessionville" was in common use by the time of the battle, and we know there was no "Battle of Riversville." All we can do is accept that the origin of this very curious name is "shrouded in legend."

\*    \*    \*

"History," as historian E. Milby Burton has written, "cannot be changed but to some extent, it can be reconstructed." Thus, the purpose of this book is not to rewrite the story of the Battle of Secessionville. Patrick Brennan has told that story well. But additional sources of information have become available since the publication of Brennan's book. Fresh eyes on the earlier sources, combined with a look at the newer ones, should, in the hope of the author, clarify some aspects of the story and draw further attention to this small, but potentially very significant, fight and give readers a fuller understanding of what took place.

# Charleston's Back Door

## CHAPTER ONE

*FALL 1861–SPRING 1862*

The Stono River was the key to Charleston, South Carolina.

The British knew this in 1780 and took advantage of the knowledge during the campaign, which ultimately gave them the city in May of that year.

Control of the Stono allowed an attacker to bypass all the defenses at the entrance to Charleston Harbor. At the time of the American War of Independence, that meant just the first iteration of Fort Moultrie, a then-unnamed palmetto log structure whose garrison repulsed an attack by the British fleet on June 28, 1776. It was that repulse that prompted the British to seek an alternate way into the city when they returned four years later.

By the time of the Civil War, however, the harbor defenses included a newer, stronger Fort Moultrie plus the brand new Fort Sumter and numerous earthworks and other batteries constructed around the harbor entrance on Sullivan's, Morris, and James Islands and within the harbor itself. It was understood that whoever controlled the Stono, and therefore could ignore the main harbor defenses, also could control James Island. And whoever controlled James Island effectively controlled the back door to Charleston.

James Island, therefore, according to a *New York Times* correspondent, "has been deemed by the rebels, and rightly too, as a place requiring much attention." In addition to allowing the unopposed landing of troops directly onto the western portion

**This view, where the Wappoo flows into the Stono, looks westward. The photo was taken just north of the site of Fort Pemberton.** (cm)

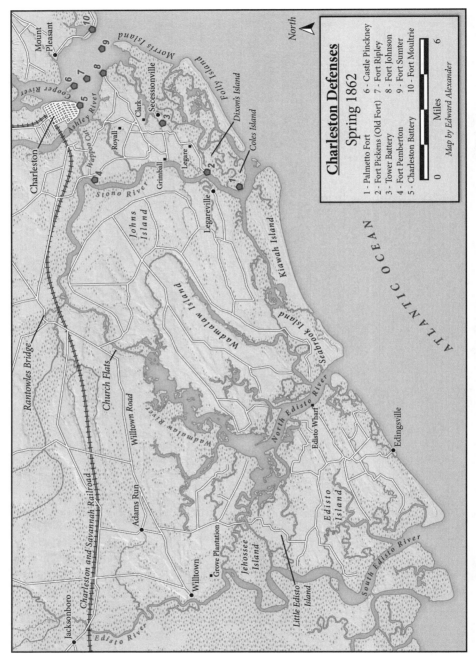

**CHARLESTON DEFENSES—Key defensive positions early in the war east of the Edisto River. Note particularly the numbered positions on James Island and in Charleston Harbor.**

of James Island, controlling the Stono also meant that a naval force could steam up the river, then cross into Charleston Harbor via the Wappoo Cut. Wappo Creek, a narrow, twisting stream, had, by 1861, been widened and straightened, connecting the Stono and Ashley Rivers. The Ashley, of course, is one of the two rivers, the other being the Cooper, which form the peninsula on which lies Charleston itself. (It was popular among the 19th-century society ladies of Charleston to declare proudly that their city sat on the site where the Ashley and Cooper Rivers came together to form the Atlantic Ocean.)

In any case, an infantry force moving eastward across James Island toward the harbor could be covered for much of its passage by the naval fire from vessels in the cut. Were the Federals to successfully accomplish this move, Charleston would virtually be in their hands.

And the Yankees absolutely wanted to take Charleston, perhaps even more for its symbolic, rather than its strategic, value. General George McClellan expressed this sentiment when he wrote early in the war that "the greatest moral effect would be produced by the reduction of Charleston and its defenses. There the rebellion had its birth; there the unnatural hatred of our Government is most intense; there is the center of the boasted power and courage of the rebels."

The Confederates certainly understood the value of this shortcut because they had been using the Ashley-Wappoo-Stono route to move troops down to Coles Island and other spots near the mouth of the river. They had been doing so ever since they began fortifying the Stono's eastern bank early in the war.

With no real navy of their own and the sting of the Union navy's capture of Port Royal in November

A sketch shows the approximate appearance of the original palmetto log fort on Sullivan's Island. (pcc)

**The Confederate works on the opposite side of the river were attacked by Union forces on January 1, 1862.** (loc)

of 1861 still fresh in their minds, Southern leaders would have known and feared that the Federals would discover the value of the Stono and be able to control it. Not surprisingly, the Federals did just that, which explains why their one attempt to take Charleston by land, half-hearted and poorly managed, eventually settled on controlling the Stono and using James Island as the jumping-off point.

*   *   *

The entrance to the Stono River from the Atlantic Ocean is the Stono Inlet. It lies roughly 10 miles southwest of Charleston Harbor between two barrier islands, Folly to the northeast and Kiawah to the southwest. Ships entering the inlet must bear slightly northwest for about two miles before turning north into the southward-flowing Stono.

From south to north along the east bank of the river lay Coles Island, Dixon's Island, Battery Island,

and Sol Legare Island. All of these are just relatively high spots in the marsh and mud along the river's east bank. They all lie between the larger James Island to the north and Folly Island to the south. Today, if driving from James Island across Sol Legare and then to the river landing at Battery Island where Union forces first came ashore, one sees no clear dividing line. It looks just like what it is; one extensive swamp. Indeed, one might realistically refer to the entire area, including Folly and Morris Islands, as a kind of Greater James Island, with each segment separated by low-lying marshes and narrow waterways. One historian colorfully referred to it as "a jigsaw puzzle of real estate."

At the time of the war, there were causeways connecting those high spots. Today's modern roads have, by and large, eliminated any distinction. There also were very few trees, all the available land having been cleared for agriculture, so that lookouts high up in the crow's nests of the Union ships on the Stono could see Secessionville some five miles away.

All of this explains why the Federal forces wanted—indeed, needed—James Island for their proposed advance on Charleston. But how did they get there? Where did they come from? And why did the strategy evolve as it did? The road map of the Union advance started many months earlier and hundreds of miles to the north. So, looking back at the timeline will explain how the Union forces under Maj. Gen. David Hunter got to Battery Island on June 2, 1862—the date that was the effective beginning of the land campaign, which eventually came to grief at Secessionville.

**Du Pont's failure to force his way into Charleston Harbor with nine ironclads in April 1863 led to his dismissal from command. He died on June 23, 1865.** (loc)

\*   \*   \*

In the autumn of 1861, President Lincoln, in consultation with and on the advice of the Navy Department, decided the South Atlantic Blockading Squadron needed a suitable base from which to conduct its operations along the Atlantic coast of the Confederacy. Its existing bases at Hampton Roads, Virginia, and Key West, Florida, were too far north and south, respectively, to be effective. Newly promoted Flag Officer Samuel F. Du Pont was given command of an expedition designed to take and secure such a base. The target was Port Royal, South Carolina.

**Brig. Gen. David Hunter replaced Brig. Gen. Thomas Sherman in command of Union army forces at Port Royal.** (loc)

Brig. Gen. Thomas W. Sherman, nicknamed "Tim," served at Fort Moultrie from 1842–44. (loc)

Du Pont had spent most of his life in the navy, serving in the fleet since receiving a midshipman's appointment from President Madison in 1815 at the age of 12. He had a distinguished career, especially during the Mexican War, and he was a highly respected officer. As such, he was an obvious choice to command the expedition to Port Royal.

Port Royal Sound had a protected harbor with space enough to provide anchorage for a vast fleet. It also offered one other significant advantage: it could be directly approached through any of three deep-water channels. Approaching vessels need not worry about running aground on a shallow bar as they did when entering Charleston Harbor some 70 sea miles to the northeast.

However, the expedition was not a preliminary move for an attack on Charleston. Its sole purpose was to establish the much-needed naval base. The accompanying troops went as a protective garrison for that base.

Sailing from Hampton Roads on October 29, 1861, Du Pont's fleet was the largest ever assembled in the United States. It consisted of 14 vessels of war and 63 supply and transport ships carrying horses, artillery, ammunition, rations, clothing, camp equipment, coal, spare parts, and Brig. Gen. Thomas W. Sherman's army assault force of some 12,000 men.

Sherman graduated in the West Point Class of 1836, ranking 18th in a class of 49. Among his classmates were Montgomery Meigs and George C. Thomas. He was no relation to the better known William Tecumseh Sherman, though the two were acquainted and had served together briefly at Fort Moultrie in 1846.

Two recently constructed but unfinished and poorly armed earthworks defended the entrance to Port Royal Sound. Fort Walker (named for Confederate Secretary of War Leroy Pope Walker) sat on Hilton Head Island to the south, and Fort Beauregard (named for the general) was situated three miles away on the southwest tip of Eddings Island (sometimes considered part of neighboring St. Helena Island) known as Bay Point. These Confederate installations were inadequately armed with largely obsolete and relatively short-range artillery because the larger Columbiad-type weapons planned for the forts simply were unavailable at the time. The two forts mounted a total of 39 guns, only about half of which could

even hope to hit the ships of the attacking Union fleet, much less to inflict serious damage.

**Hunter made his headquarters at Hilton Head, SC.** (loc)

Also available to the Confederates was a small naval force under the command of Commodore Josiah Tattnall. Tattnall had served in the Old Navy since the War of 1812 and was a highly regarded officer, considered by those who knew him to be "chivalrous, genial, unassuming, and heroic." As a Georgian, however, he resigned his commission and went with his home state when the war began. His son, Marine Lieutenant John R. F. Tattnall, followed him and joined the Confederate States Marine Corps. Promoted therein to captain, the younger Tattnall commanded the Confederate Marines in Savannah and served for a time as an aide-de-camp to General Lee.

Commodore Tattnall's so-called "Mosquito Fleet" consisted of five small steamers, *Savannah*, *Resolute*, *Sampson*, *Lady Davis*, and *Huntress*, all hastily converted to gunships and mounting a grand total of

This pre-war image shows Josiah Tattnall, who would later become commander of the Confederate naval defenses of Port Royal. (nhh)

eight cannon among them. It was, to be charitable, ineffective; even more so because Huntress was absent at the time of the Port Royal fight, transporting some wounded men to Charleston.

One naval historian later wrote that Tattnall's vessels were "river boats; as men-of-war they were in every respect of the most vulnerable class." Tattnall himself once described his fleet as "all those d-----d old tubs" and threatened to sink them as mere river obstructions.

It is one of those marvelous curiosities so common in the Civil War that Brig. Gen. Thomas F. Drayton controlled the Confederate harbor defenses while his brother, Commander Percival Drayton, was the commanding officer of the USS *Pocahontas*, one of the warships in Flag Officer Du Pont's fleet. Onshore, Brig. Gen. Drayton commanded the Third Military District of South Carolina. He had graduated from West Point in 1828, finishing 28th of 33 in the class, five places below his classmate, Jefferson Davis. General Drayton also happened to be president of the Charleston and Savannah Railroad. His brother, Commander Drayton, was a career naval officer, having been commissioned as a midshipman in 1827 when he was 15 years old.

With the departure of the Union fleet from Hampton Roads, Du Pont worried about keeping his "heterogeneous squadron" together during the voyage. His concern was warranted because, as with any convoy, the slowest ship's speed and seaworthiness limited the group's overall speed. The weather did not help. A powerful storm off Cape Hatteras scattered the ships over a wide expanse of the Atlantic on November 1. Three ships were lost, and a fourth was forced to turn back. The battered fleet did not reassemble until late on November 4.

Du Pont, with his flagship, the USS *Wabash*, was among the first to arrive at the rendezvous off Port Royal following the storm. The relatively new *Wabash*, a 300-foot, 4,800-ton, "steam-screw frigate," had been commissioned in August 1856. Mounting more than 40 large Dahlgren guns, she was a formidable vessel of war.

With the bulk of the fleet arriving by November 4, Du Pont ordered his captains to make the necessary repairs and prepare their ships for the coming fight. That fight began about 9:00 a.m. on November 7. This time, the weather was perfect.

The warships advanced in column into Port Royal Sound on the incoming tide and began pounding both forts with their heavy guns. Once well into the sound, the vessels turned to port and made their way back between the forts but closer to Fort Walker. Now moving against the tide, the steam-powered warships slowed down, but the weight of their metal told against the weaker Confederate force, and even at the reduced speed, their movement frustrated the poorly trained rebel gunners. Several of the Union vessels moved out of the line and anchored in a position that allowed them to fire on the flank of Fort Walker.

On reaching the mouth of the Sound, the remaining ships in the formation repeated the loop a second time, then a third. While this took place, the small Confederate flotilla advanced as if to enter the fray, but several Union gunboats, specially assigned to keep it at bay, deterred the attempt. Tattnall's little navy had no chance and withdrew to the shelter of Hilton Head Island.

Union firepower overwhelmed the two forts, and within four hours, the Confederate defenders abandoned Fort Walker, then Fort Beauregard. Shortly thereafter, Du Pont sent a force of Marines and sailors ashore to secure them. When the landing parties had accomplished this, they turned both forts over to the

**The USS *Wabash* served as the flagship of the South Atlantic Blockading Squadron early in the war. Decommissioned and recommissioned several times, she was not stricken from the navy list until 1912.** (loc)

General Robert E. Lee's four months as commander of the Department of South Carolina and Georgia was a series of frustrations that nonetheless produced a solid defensive strategy for the area. (loc)

army, which had, in the interim, landed in force. Fort Walker was renamed Fort Welles after Union Secretary of the Navy Gideon Welles. Fort Beauregard became Fort Seward after William Seward, President Lincoln's Secretary of State.

The Federals had successfully established a beach head on the South Carolina coast, a beach head which included most of the Low Country islands between Charleston and Savannah.

Having secured the area, Brig. Gen. Sherman and Flag Officer Du Pont cooperated in the construction of a joint army-navy base. Port Royal became a major Federal installation and the home of the South Atlantic Blockading Squadron for the remainder of the war. Interestingly, Commander William Reynolds, brother of Union Maj. Gen. John F. Reynolds, commanded the naval depot portion of this joint base for much of the war.

*   *   *

When Brig. Gen. Drayton's Confederate forces abandoned the forts, they withdrew to positions farther inland and closer to the railroad. Within two months, they would face the invading Yankees again. Though a matter of necessity for Drayton's troops, this withdrawal into the interior fit into the eventual defensive plans of the overall Confederate commander, General Robert E. Lee, who had been appointed to command the Department of South Carolina and Georgia on November 5, only two days before Du Pont's attack on Port Royal. Lee arrived on the scene to find out that Port Royal had fallen to the enemy. He would hold his command for only four months before being called back to Richmond and replaced by Brig. Gen. John C. Pemberton on March 14, 1862.

Lee's inability to match the mobility which the navy gave to the Union forces put him at an enormous disadvantage. Understanding that he could not successfully oppose the navy's powerful guns, Lee felt he had no real choice except to abandon the sea islands and concentrate his meager forces further inland to protect the vital Charleston and Savannah Railroad which gave him some mobility of his own. "I am in favor of abandoning all exposed points," he wrote in February 1862, "as far as possible within reach of the enemy's gunboats and of taking interior positions, where we can meet on more equal terms."

Holding the railroad, he believed, was his only chance to hold Charleston and Savannah.

At this point, the new commander had only about 7,000 poorly trained and poorly equipped troops to protect more than one hundred miles of railroad. He eventually would get strong reinforcements, but he still was not optimistic. Thinking of his recent unsuccessful experience in West Virginia, Lee described his situation as "another forlorn hope expedition." However, his defensive strategy at least forced Union troops to advance beyond the cover of naval gunfire support if they wanted to take the offensive.

Following the successful assault on Port Royal, Union offensive activities on land in this region virtually ceased. The goal to capture Port Royal and establish a base had been accomplished. Extensive inland operations were not objectives at that time. The Federals seemed unsure what to do next and were not in a position to do much anyway. Moreover, both services badly needed resupply. The army clearly needed both cavalry and field artillery if it wanted to maneuver, and it had none of the former and little of the latter. The navy suffered from a severe shortage of the powerful 11-inch shells, which had proven so valuable in reducing the Port Royal forts.

On top of it all, Maj. Gen. George McClellan, the Union Army's overall commander, lay seriously ill with typhoid fever for long periods during the winter of 1861-62. McClellan simply did not see much of the communication his office received from Brig. Gen. Sherman, so Sherman waited with growing frustration for instructions.

At one point, Sherman practically begged McClellan to respond. Writing on January 2, he said, "The time has come to act; every day's delay now is a sad loss." He finished with this plea: "You, general, are to be the savior of this country, if it is saved. Let me aid you in the work." The whole tone of this communication bordered on desperation.

\*   \*   \*

On January 1, 1862, Brig. Gen. Isaac Stevens's troops, most of whom would be involved in the Secessionville fight nearly six months later, engaged in a hotly contested series of skirmishes with the Confederates at and around the Port Royal (or Coosaw) Ferry, some 25 miles above Hilton Head.

Having succeeded General Lee in command of his department, Maj. Gen. John C. Pemberton continued Lee's defensive policies but received criticism for this from civilian leaders and his subordinates. (loc)

With the arrival of General Benham, with whom he did not get along, as his immediate commander, Isaac Stevens unsuccessfully sought a transfer. (loc)

Though generally referred to as the battle of Port Royal Ferry, the action started as a raid by Union forces on several Confederate batteries on the interior waterways opposite Hilton Head Island, some still under construction. The ferry battery was only one of the new fortifications. The ferry site itself was located at Stuart's Point on the road from Beaufort to Pocataligo, the railroad depot which served as the headquarters for the Fourth Military District (SC) commanded by Brig. Gen. Pemberton (soon to be replaced by Brig. Gen. Maxcy Gregg when Pemberton himself replaced Lee in overall command). Stuart's Point is about two miles east of where the modern US 21 highway bridge crosses the Coosaw on its way to Beaufort.

Several companies of Col. Daniel Leasure's 100th Pennsylvania (known as the Roundheads) attacked the ferry site. Stevens's brigade, augmented by two additional regiments, targeted the other assault sites, which were at various points along the Coosaw and on Whale Branch, a connecting waterway between the Broad and Coosaw Rivers.

The Union offensive was a combined arms operation with the naval force under Capt. Christopher R.P. Rodgers, consisting of five gunboats—*Ottawa, Pembina, Seneca, E.B. Hale*, and *Ellen*—and several armed launches, providing transportation and fire support for the soldiers. Du Pont had great confidence in Rodgers

**A plantation house in Beaufort served as Thomas Sherman's headquarters.** (loc)

and wrote to his wife that the commander's presence on this escapade "relieves me much for I know where he is that all will be done that is right."

In addition to the navy, the Federal forces included the 8th Michigan, the 47th, 49th, and 79th New York, the 50th and 100th Pennsylvania infantry regiments, and Battery E of the 3rd U.S. Artillery, all commanded by Brig. Gen. Stevens. These troops faced off against portions of the 12th and 14th South Carolina infantry regiments, a section of Leake's (Virginia) Battery, and about 40 assorted South Carolina cavalrymen on the Confederate side, all under the immediate command of Col. James Jones of the 14th South Carolina. Portions of the 8th and 16th Tennessee infantry regiments remained in reserve but were not engaged.

**Commander Rodgers was one of Admiral Du Pont's favorite and most trusted subordinate officers.** (loc)

The gunboats landed troops near the ferry, then shelled the earthworks, driving the Confederates away and causing them to burn stores of cotton and corn to prevent their capture. It also cost the Southern forces a 12-pounder which was knocked into a ditch by a shot fired from one of the gunboats and had to be spiked and abandoned. Union troops sporadically pursued the Rebels for short distances before withdrawing to the transports.

Though a Union victory resulted, the laurels belonged more to the navy than the army. Each time the Federal troops advanced beyond the range of the navy's big guns, the Confederates drove them back. Each time the Confederates tried to push the advantage, the gunboats forced them, in turn, to retire. However, neither Brig. Gen. Isaac Stevens in his official reports, nor Hazard Stevens in his biography of his father, gave much credit to the navy, a fact which irritated Lt. John S. Barnes, in command of the gunboat *E.B. Hale*. Barnes wrote, somewhat sardonically, that the navy was ordered to "cooperate with the Army, which nowadays means to do all the hard fighting and let the Army take the benefit and the glory of it."

But as Brig. Gen. Stevens's aide, Lt. William T. Lusk, admitted, "The fact is the frightful effects of the explosions of the 11-inch shell which some of our gunboats carry have produced a great panic among the land forces of South Carolina."

The ultimate effect of this fight was to turn the Coosaw River into a hard boundary between the contending forces. This prevented any Confederate counterattack on Hilton Head or Beaufort bottled up the Union forces that were not in any shape to move further inland in a significant way.

The action around the Port Royal Ferry proved to be the high point of Federal army-navy cooperation for the next two years or more. Inter-service and inter-personal rivalries within the individual services became pronounced from here on, with the effects to be seen in the coming months.

Inter-personal rivalries probably affected the state-centered volunteer army more than the navy. But perhaps the more important overall problems were the structural and organizational deficiencies within a navy which never really had developed a strategy of fleet operations as, for example, the British Navy had. The American Navy, instead, had depended on the tactics of single ship cruising and commerce raiding, which had served it reasonably well against the British, the French, and the Barbary States in the earlier years of its existence.

This lack of consistent, synchronized fleet training limited the navy's ability to react in an institutional way to the needs of a large army. That meant army-navy operations were not joint operations in the modern sense, but rather were cooperative arrangements. If the individual army and navy commanders got along personally, then inter-service cooperation was more likely to be possible.

This deficiency remained with the navy until almost the 20th century when the strategic thinking of Alfred Thayer Mahan, and the personal energy of Assistant Secretary of the Navy Theodore Roosevelt, took hold. That said, it also is true that West Point did not teach its cadets an appreciation of the importance of naval operations. For too many army officers, the navy existed primarily to transport and supply their men.

Nonetheless, the navy kept busy during the months following the Port Royal Ferry fighting, partly by exploring and charting the many shallow waterways along the coast above and below Port Royal and partly by taking several coastal towns, including Fernandina and Jacksonville in Florida and Brunswick in Georgia.

However, Savannah soon became the focal point for Du Pont and Sherman. Both men wanted to take that Georgia city, but Fort Pulaski kept them from doing so. Situated on Cockspur Island, the fort effectively guarded both channels of the Savannah River, where it flowed eastward into the Atlantic. Throughout

January 1862, the navy explored the waterways south of the river, looking for a way to bypass the fort, but none of the possibilities seemed suitable.

The idea of a *coup de main* against Savannah gradually became less attractive. Major General McClellan's recovery and correspondence catch-up forced the plan's abandonment altogether. McClellan's interest focused on Maj. Gen. Ambrose Burnside's Hatteras Expedition rather than on events at Port Royal, and "Little Mac" responded to Sherman on February 14 with instructions to concentrate on reducing Fort Pulaski because "under present circumstances the siege and capture of Savannah do not promise results commensurate with the sacrifices necessary." Savannah finally would fall to the forces of the other General Sherman almost three years later.

Capt. Quincy Adams Gillmore was among the first to understand the power of rifled artillery. He oversaw the 30-hour barrage that forced the surrender of Fort Pulaski. (loc)

McClellan's decision disappointed Sherman, but he still had to deal with Fort Pulaski. In February, the army had begun building batteries on Tybee Island and other areas in the vicinity to cut Fort Pulaski off from Savannah. Once this was accomplished, the question was whether to attack the fort directly or simply let it wither on the vine, starving out the garrison. That low-key siege process likely would have taken 6 to 10 months, depending on how well the Confederates had managed to hoard and ration their food and supplies.

Unwilling to wait, General Sherman turned to his chief engineer, Capt. Quincy Adams Gillmore to find a solution, and Gillmore did. Born only a week before John Quincy Adams was inaugurated as president and named after him, Gillmore had graduated at the top of his West Point Class of 1849. An imaginative engineer, he was among the first to realize what large caliber rifled artillery could do to brick walls. He had eleven batteries erected and armed with heavy mortars and rifled guns. Together, these would make short work of what most artillerists at the time believed to be a virtually impregnable Fort Pulaski.

Sherman would not be around to see the success, however, as he was relieved by the War Department and replaced by Brig. Gen. David Hunter only two weeks before the Fort Pulaski garrison was forced to surrender.

# 10 V 76

# THE SEIZURE OF THE *PLANTER*

Early on May 13, 1862, Robert Smalls, an enslaved harbor pilot aboard the *Planter*, seized the 149-ft. Confederate transport from a wharf just east of here. He and six enslaved crewmen took the vessel before dawn when its captain, pilot, and engineer were ashore. Smalls guided the ship through the channel, past Fort Sumter, and out to sea, delivering it to the Federal fleet which was blockading the harbor.

(Continued on other side)

SPONSORED BY HISTORIC CHARLESTON FOUNDATION AND THE AFRICAN AMERICAN HISTORICAL ALLIANCE, 2012

# The Great Escape

## CHAPTER TWO

### MAY 12–13, 1862

In a way, it all began with Robert Smalls. General Thomas W. Sherman and then his successor, Gen. David Hunter, had been thinking about how best to take Charleston for some time. Of course, there had been preparations made, troops moved about, camps established, supplies stockpiled, and reconnaissances conducted. But what Smalls did when he fled from slavery to freedom, bringing his family and several friends with him, began the sequence of events that led to the battle of Secessionville. Smalls's actions prompted General Hunter to begin seriously preparing for a land assault on James Island, long understood as the key to Charleston.

Robert Smalls was born on April 5, 1839, in the slave quarters behind the home of Henry McKee of Beaufort, South Carolina, some 75 miles south of Charleston.

His mother's name was Lydia Polite, but his father's identity is unknown. Smalls may have been his father's name or a name of his own choosing; he never was clear about that for the record. Nor did his mother ever reveal the identity of his father, at least, not to anyone but him. Occasional speculation that his father was white, possibly one of the McKee men, remains only speculation.

Robert's boyhood was unexceptional for the time. Lydia cooked for the McKee family and may have been a nanny to the McKee children, so her son became a houseboy in the McKee household. He did what young slave boys in that position normally would have been expected to do. He ran errands

**A state historical marker along Charleston's Battery tells the story of the fabled steamer Planter.** (cm)

**Robert Smalls was a former slave whose escape provided Union forces with the information they needed to begin the campaign that resulted in the battle of Secessionville.** (nhh)

and performed useful chores for his master. He was, according to his biographer, Cate Lineberry, "smart, capable, and well-liked by the McKee family."

In 1851, at the age of 12, Robert was sent to Charleston, where he seems to have lived with Eliza Russell Ancrum, a relative of the McKee family and was hired out to work. His wages would have gone either to his master or Miss Ancrum for his upkeep, a fairly common practice at that time.

Smalls first worked as a waiter at the Planter's Hotel, an amusing bit of irony given his later association with the *Planter*, the vessel which played such a major role in his life and, indeed, made him famous.

He then took a job with the Charleston Gas Light Company as a lamplighter and later worked on the Charleston docks as a stevedore. Eventually, he became a crewman on a local harbor vessel, where he learned to hand, reef, steer, and even repair sails and rigging and, significantly, to navigate. During the 1850s, he became a highly qualified seaman, boat handler, and harbor pilot, skills which turned out to be his ticket to freedom.

On December 24, 1856, Christmas Eve, at the Henry McKee home in Beaufort, seventeen-year-old Robert Smalls took a wife. Hannah Jones was in her mid-30s and already had three children of her own, including an infant boy. It was a curious union. Lineberry writes that Robert's attachment to Hannah was genuine but that he had a very practical reason for marriage as well. As he later explained, he wanted "to have a wife to prevent me from running around—to have somebody to do for me and to keep me." It sounds like he wanted a mother as much as a wife. Hannah's reasons for agreeing to the marriage are unclear.

Two years later, the couple had a daughter, Elizabeth Lydia. Shortly after the child's birth, Robert asked Hannah's owner, a local banker named Samuel Kingman, if he could purchase her freedom. Kingman agreed and set Hannah's price at $800. Saving that much would take years, but Robert and Hannah managed to put aside a little each month for that purpose.

Then came the war, and Smalls was hired as a deck hand aboard the *Planter*. The *Planter* was a relatively new vessel, a sidewheel steamer. At 147 feet and just over 300 tons, but drawing less than four

Cotton bales loaded down on the *Planter.* (loc)

feet of water, she hauled men and materiel around the harbor and through the shallow waterways in the area. Her owner, John Ferguson, leased her to the Confederate government, which armed her with a 32-pounder forward and a 24-pounder aft.

By the fall of 1861, Smalls often stood at the helm of the vessel. Also by then, Hannah had given birth to their second child, a boy named Robert Smalls, Jr. who, rather curiously, was called "Beauregard." One wonders if his nickname resulted from someone's mischievous sense of humor.

On May 12, 1862, the *Planter* went to Coles Island at the entrance of the Stono River. Her task was to load four heavy artillery pieces which had been dismounted from batteries there to be transported to

Fort Ripley, a battery built on a man-made island in the harbor about halfway between Castle Pinckney and Fort Johnson.

Completely gone now, Fort Ripley sat on a sand bar in shallow water known as the Middle Ground. The fort had been constructed by first building a crib of heavy timber, which then was filled with debris from the great fire that had destroyed much of downtown Charleston on December 11-12, 1861. This provided the foundation for the roughly 150-foot square structure. Designed for four guns, the fort may never have had that many, and when the Federals re-occupied it on February 18, 1865, it had a "quaker gun" in place. It was so small that there was no room to house the garrison, so the men quartered on a boat moored at the back side of the battery.

At least one of the guns removed from Coles Island and intended for Fort Ripley had been part of Fort Sumter's original armament and was relocated by the Confederates. It later was identified by some damage to the muzzle where it had been hit by a Confederate shot during the bombardment in April of 1861. It soon would be back in Union hands.

The *Planter*'s crew loaded and secured the guns on the ship, then returned to her usual berth at the Southern Wharf on the Cooper River (near today's Historic Charleston Foundation office on lower East Bay Street) for the night. They would deliver the guns the following day, but not to Fort Ripley.

**Brig. Gen. Roswell S. Ripley, namesake of Fort Ripley, commanded the defenses of Charleston Harbor for much of the war.** (loc)

About 3:00 a.m. on May 13, Smalls set his plan in motion. The vessel's captain, Charles J. Relyea, and his two white crewmen decided, against standing military orders, to spend the night ashore with their families. Relyea left the *Planter* in the charge of Smalls and the six other black crewmen. He had done this before without incident.

Captain Relyea was something of a hard-luck sailor. In December 1860, he had been in command of the *General Clinch* when that South Carolina gunboat patrolled the channel between Forts Moultrie and Sumter to prevent Major Robert Anderson from moving his Union garrison from the former to the latter. Anderson evaded him and successfully got his men to Sumter. Relyea's hard luck continued with the *Planter*. (It is yet another marvelous Civil War coincidence that the *General Clinch*, whose purpose was to blow Major Anderson's force out of the water if necessary, had been named for former U.S. Army

General Duncan L. Clinch, who happened to be Anderson's father-in-law.)

The *Planter*'s crew fired up the boilers, making no attempt to be particularly quiet about it but going about the work as if they were conducting regular business so as not to attract undue attention from guards on the wharves. When all was ready, Smalls raised the Stars and Bars, blew the whistle per the prescribed procedure, and backed out of the slip. However, instead of heading for the harbor entrance, he turned the *Planter* upriver and touched briefly at the North Atlantic Wharf several hundred yards away (roughly mid-way up the length of today's Waterfront Park). There, he picked up his wife and children along with several of the crewmen's families, a total of eight adults and three children, all of whom had been hiding aboard another harbor steamer, the *Etiwan*. Only then did Smalls, his crew, and their families begin their dash for freedom.

The *Etiwan* is notable for having been involved in two other events of local historical significance. On June 4, 1862, she carried Union prisoners to captivity in Charleston following the skirmishing on Sol Legare Island. And, on August 29, 1863, she moored next to the submarine *H. L. Hunley* when that vessel accidentally sank in 42 feet of water, killing five of her crew.

For about the next two hours, the *Planter* followed all the rules as she slowly made her way toward the gauntlet of Fort Sumter and Fort Moultrie. Smalls, wearing Captain Relyea's coat and trademark wide-brimmed straw hat, knew all the proper signals necessary to pass each of the Confederate installations in the harbor. Luckily, no one sounded an alarm.

Approaching the narrow opening in the obstacles which the Confederates had used to block the harbor entrance, the *Planter* had to pass within point-blank range of the lower tier of Sumter's guns. At this critical moment, Smalls's luck held again. He sounded the proper signal on the whistle, received an acknowledgment and a friendly wave from a guard atop the wall, and headed into the Atlantic and freedom. The guards at Fort Sumter seem to have mistaken the *Planter* for the regular picket ship which patrolled near the harbor entrance.

One more problem remained to be overcome, however. The Union blockading ships might well mistake the *Planter* for an attacking Confederate

Deceased before the war, Brig. Gen. Duncan L. Clinch was Maj. Robert Anderson's father-in-law and the namesake of the South Carolina state vessel that unsuccessfully attempted to prevent Anderson from transferring his men from Ft. Moultrie to Ft. Sumter. (loc)

**Cmdr. Enoch G. Parrott fought in the Mexican War. He later helped destroy the Norfolk Navy Yard at the beginning of the Civil War and participated in both attacks on Fort Fisher, North Carolina.** (nhh)

warship or possibly a blockade runner. What to do if the Union Navy opened fire? All their planning and effort, not to mention their lives, could end in the flash of a broadside. To prevent this, Smalls had the Confederate flag lowered and a large, white bed sheet hoisted in its place. The sun started rising, but heavy fog obscured the scene, so everyone waited tensely.

Lieutenant John Nickels of the USS *Onward* first saw the strange vessel coming toward him and sensibly ordered his men to battle stations. Fortunately for those aboard the *Planter*, however, Nickels saw the bed sheet and held his fire. He hailed the vessel and ordered it to heave to or be fired upon. Shouts of joy from the men and women aboard her greeted him. Smalls explained who they were and what they were doing, then asked for a United States flag to hoist. Nickels came aboard with a flag, promptly raised it, and Smalls presented himself, the others, and the vessel to the U.S. Navy.

Nickels reported the incident to Commander Enoch G. Parrott, temporarily in command of the Charleston blockading squadron (and, coincidentally, a first cousin of Robert P. Parrott, inventor of the famed rifled artillery pieces that bear his name). Placing a warrant officer and several sailors from the USS *Augusta* aboard the *Planter*, the Federals then sent her to Port Royal and instructed Smalls to report to Flag Officer Du Pont.

Later in the morning, as the *Planter* made its way toward Port Royal, escorted by the USS *Ottawa*, she passed—and Smalls surely saw—Coles Island, where on the previous morning he and his crew had retrieved the four artillery pieces intended for Fort Ripley, but which now were in the hands of the U.S. Navy. Just as Smalls could see Coles Island, the men of the 24th South Carolina stationed there could see him or, at least, see the *Planter*. Brigadier General Gist reported that his men spotted the ship heading south about 11:00 that morning. No doubt they felt considerably less satisfaction at seeing him than he did at seeing them.

The *Planter*'s escape, amazing as it was on its own, especially galled the Confederates as a similar escape had been made only two weeks before. On the night of April 27, some fifteen slaves had stolen General Ripley's barge (an oared boat, sometimes called a gig, used as his personal conveyance). The men made their way undetected out of the harbor just as Smalls later did and turned themselves and the boat over to the Union Navy early the next morning. Their action alerted the Confederates to the possibility of such things happening, but they apparently believed it was unlikely to happen again. This was not unreasonable. It was one thing, after all, to steal a rowboat, but quite another to abscond with a nearly 150-foot long, steam-powered gunboat.

It also is worth noting, as a matter of historical curiosity, that another ship was added to Flag Officer Du Pont's flotilla about the same time as the *Planter*. This was the yacht *America*, after whom the America's Cup was named. The yacht had gone through several owners following her famous 1851 victory in a race around the Isle of Wight before becoming the property of the Confederacy early in the war. She had a brief, but not particularly noteworthy, career as a blockade runner. As a sleek racing yacht designed for speed, she did not have much storage space in her hold for the kinds of cargoes which made blockade running so potentially profitable. The Confederates scuttled her near Jacksonville, Florida, when that city fell to Union forces. The Federals raised and repaired her. On May 17, Du Pont wrote to the Navy Department asking for her because "I find I can make her very useful here as a blockading vessel." His request was approved, and she became part of the South Atlantic Blockading Squadron until assigned to other duties in May 1863.

The racing yacht *America* served as part of the South Atlantic Blockading Squadron in 1862–63. (nhh)

Aside from giving the *Planter* and six artillery pieces (two mounted on the ship; four transported) to the Union Navy, Smalls also provided critical intelligence and signals information to an astonished Du Pont during their conversation. He revealed the Confederate abandonment of Coles Island and the fact that the Rebels recently had sent large numbers of troops to Virginia and Tennessee. This changed everything, and within a matter of days, the Federals began to confirm the information. They sent ships past the former Confederate works on Coles Island and began reconnoitering and marking the Stono river channel in preparation for a landing.

But this exploit was just the beginning for Robert Smalls.

Du Pont first urged the government to award Smalls and the others a share of the prize money for the *Planter*. As civilians, they normally would not have been eligible for this type of payment which traditionally went to sailors involved in capturing enemy vessels. In this case, however, in recognition of what they had done, Congress acted quickly. A bill was prepared, passed, and signed into law by President Lincoln on May 30, by which Smalls and the others received some financial reward for their exploit. Smalls received $1,500, which he later used to help set himself up in business.

The reverse side of the state historical marker about the *Planter* concludes the story. (cm)

10 V 76

THE SEIZURE OF THE *PLANTER*
(Continued from other side)

Northern and Southern newspapers called this feat "bold" and "daring." Smalls and his crew, a crewman on another ship, and eight other enslaved persons including Smalls's wife, Hannah, and three children, won their freedom by it. Smalls (1839-1915) was appointed captain of the *Planter* by a U.S. Army contract in 1863. A native of Beaufort, he was later a state legislator and then a five-term U.S. Congressman.

SPONSORED BY HISTORIC CHARLESTON FOUNDATION
AND THE AFRICAN AMERICAN HISTORICAL ALLIANCE, 2012

Du Pont also hired Smalls as a civilian pilot for the navy. Smalls worked on several vessels during the war, even participating in the fighting on April 7, 1863, as pilot of the ill-fated USS *Keokuk* when that ironclad and several others attempted to force their way into Charleston Harbor and received a battering from Confederate guns at Fort Sumter and the batteries on Sullivan's Island. The attack ended in a complete failure, and the Federals withdrew. The *Keokuk* eventually sank.

A few weeks later, the Confederates salvaged the *Keokuk*'s two 11-inch Dahlgren guns right out from under the noses of the Union Navy and incorporated them into Charleston's defenses. One of those

The gun in the background is one of two 11-inch Dahlgren guns salvaged by the Confederates from the wreck of the USS *Keokuk* in April 1863 and mounted in the Charleston Battery to defend the city. (loc)

guns is on display today at White Point Garden in Charleston.

In November of that year, again working as a pilot aboard the *Planter*, Smalls took charge when the ship got caught in a crossfire between Union and Confederate batteries, and the captain panicked. When the captain fled below to hide in the coal bunker, Smalls assumed command and got the vessel out of harm's way. He saved the *Planter* from destruction or capture that day (saving himself from re-enslavement or death at the same time). For this, he received a formal appointment as her captain, a position he held for the remainder of the war.

Afterward, he entered politics, serving in the state legislature and the U.S. House of Representatives. He also purchased the McKee house in Beaufort where he had grown up, living there until his death on February 23, 1915.

Robert Smalls gave an important gift to the Union Army and Navy commanders. They soon began to put that gift to good use.

# *Hunter and Benham Begin to Move*

## CHAPTER THREE

### *MARCH–MAY 1862*

Brigadier General Sherman's unfairly perceived lack of activity resulted in Brig. Gen. David "Black Dave" Hunter replacing him. On March 15, 1862, War Department General Orders No. 26 redesignated General Sherman's area of operations as the Department of the South and placed the department under the command of General Hunter. It is curious that Hunter replaced Sherman on March 15 while, on the Confederate side, Pemberton had replaced Lee only a day before. The changes in their respective command structures caused tensions and problems on both sides.

Hunter arrived at Port Royal on March 31. "For the convenience of military operations and the administration of department affairs," he then divided his department into three very unequal districts. The states of South Carolina and Georgia, plus northeastern Florida, became the Northern District, commanded by Brig. Gen. Henry Washington Benham. Most of the Florida peninsula became the Southern District under Brig. Gen. John M. Brannan at Fort Zachary Taylor in Key West. The Florida panhandle became the Western District under Brig. Gen. Lewis G. Arnold at Fort Pickens in Pensacola. The two smaller districts play virtually no further role in this story.

A pre-war acquaintance and favorite of Lincoln early in the war, Hunter was born in Princeton, New Jersey, in 1802. His father, Rev. Andrew Hunter, had

**A statue of Col. Benjamin Christ overlooks the Antietam battlefield from the monument of the 50th Pennsylvania.** (lr)

**Brig. Gen. Henry Benham was a better engineer than he was an infantry officer.** (loc)

been the chaplain of the 3rd New Jersey Infantry Regiment during the American Revolution, and his maternal grandfather, Richard Stockton, had been a signer of the Declaration of Independence. As a graduate of the West Point Class of 1822, Hunter ranked among the Civil War's elder statesmen along with classmates Joseph Mansfield, Isaac Trimble, and George McCall. He finished 25th in that class of 40 cadets.

A hard-core abolitionist, the new department commander probably is best known for two things. First, his May 9, 1862, general order declared martial law in the Department of the South and freed all slaves held therein. Second is his "scorched earth" policy in the Shenandoah Valley in 1864, which included the burning of the Virginia Military Institute.

President Lincoln, not yet ready for something quite as drastic as Hunter's emancipation order, soon rescinded it, something which Hunter should have known he would do. Hunter previously had served under Brig. Gen. John C. Fremont when that officer issued a similar declaration of emancipation in Missouri and saw it rescinded. Lincoln had then fired Fremont on November 2, 1861, and named Hunter himself as Fremont's replacement in command of the Department of the West.

By April, Hunter had arrived in his new southern command and immediately allowed General Gillmore to continue the preparations to reduce Fort Pulaski. The bombardment began on April 10, and thirty hours later, it had succeeded beyond everyone's (except Gillmore's) expectations. The heavy rifles breached the nearly seven-and-a-half foot thick walls of the fort and exposed at least one of its powder magazines.

About mid-afternoon on April 11, Col. Charles Olmstead, commanding the garrison, hauled down his flag and surrendered. He did so only one day shy of the first anniversary of the bombardment of Fort Sumter. In response, First Lieutenant Horace Porter (later the personal secretary to General Grant), who had assisted Gillmore in supervising the construction of the siege batteries, exclaimed, "Pulaski is ours. Sumter is avenged!" Pulaski's fall meant that Hunter had begun his departmental command with an important victory; a victory that immediately and unequivocally rendered obsolete every masonry fort constructed in America during the previous 40 years.

The parallels between the bombardments of Forts Sumter and Pulaski are intriguing in themselves. Thirty hours for Pulaski versus 34 for Sumter. Powder magazines—exposed and endangered in both cases— became the primary justification for each fort's capitulation; and, of course, the near coincidence of the dates.

The surrender of Fort Pulaski effectively isolated Savannah and rendered it useless as a port. With that, the attentions of General Hunter and Flag Officer Du Pont logically turned to Charleston.

*    *    *

The change of command that brought General Hunter south did not please Brig. Gen. Isaac Stevens. Stevens and Sherman had forged a mutually respectful working relationship, partly because of Sherman's conditional approval of Stevens's strategic plan to take and control the Charleston and Savannah Railroad. This relationship might have continued with General Hunter but for the influence of Benham. Benham and Stevens had butted heads in the past and did not get along.

The two had known each other since West Point, where they had overlapped for two years. It is unclear, though, how well they knew each other at the Academy or what relationship they might have had as cadets. Each man graduated first in his class; Benham in 1837, Stevens in 1839. Both were assigned to the engineers, and both later achieved some distinction in the Mexican War.

In October 1849, Stevens began an assignment as Assistant Director of the United States Coast Survey under the highly respected Professor Alexander Dallas Bache and became one of the professor's close friends. At that time, the Coast Survey went through a period of rapid expansion due to the country's acquisition of California and the territories of the Southwest following the Mexican War. Stevens spent considerable time reforming and reorganizing the bureau to make it better able to cope with its increased responsibilities. Bache essentially left him alone to do this.

In 1853, Stevens resigned his commission and left the Coast Survey to take the position of Governor of the Washington Territory. Benham replaced him at the Survey and was highly critical of some of his reforms. He did not endear himself to Stevens when he claimed that Stevens had left behind a mess which he (Benham) then had to straighten out.

Stevens would not have been happy to see Benham show up at Hilton Head and surely was even less pleased to learn that his old harsh critic was now his immediate superior.

Not surprisingly, the members of Stevens' staff agreed with their commander's assessment of the new regime, including both Hunter and Benham. Lieutenant William T. Lusk, Stevens' assistant adjutant general, wrote to his mother that "we all were in the habit of abusing Genl. Sherman in old times, but with customary fickleness, wish him back again now. This last batch of General officers with the 'Great Superseder' (Hunter) at the head, is poor trash at best, so that there are few who would not rejoice to have "Uncle Tim" (Sherman) back again, notwithstanding his dyspepsia and peripatetic propensities."

The bad relationship was solidified when Benham summarily rejected Stevens's plan for a move on the railroad. Stevens had been urging such an attack at least since the previous December, but while Sherman had approved the plan in principle, he cautiously insisted that Stevens could proceed only after Fort Pulaski had fallen. As things played out, that did not occur for several months, leaving Stevens frustrated and impatient.

* * *

On December 9, 1861, Stevens wrote to Sherman asking permission "to seize the railroad crossing on Broad River and silence it by works." This occurred only a month after the Federals had taken Port Royal, showing Stevens's eagerness to exploit that success. However, he was wrong about one thing. The railroad did not cross the Broad River. It did cross both the Coosawhatchie and Tulifinny Rivers, which parallel each other about a mile and a half apart and come together about four miles south of that point to form the Broad. Stevens most likely referred to the crossing of the Coosawhatchie, as it was there that Gen. Lee had set up his headquarters.

Having presented his plan to Brig. Gen. Benham and been, in his view, dismissively rebuffed, Stevens became distraught and began looking for a way out. He wrote to his friend from their old Washington Territory days, Senator James Nesmith of Oregon, asking Nesmith to help him find a different assignment.

In the meantime, he persisted with Benham and thought at one point that he had gotten Benham's permission to execute his plan for the attack on the railroad. But Benham's permission extended only to allowing Stevens to take one regiment on a quick, day-long raid up in that general direction. Though not remotely what Stevens wanted, he tried to make the best of it, hoping to burn the bridge near Pocotaligo at least.

Stevens's persistence had not gained Benham's permission, however. Benham had decided much earlier to incorporate part of Stevens's idea into his overall plan to take Charleston. He did not let Stevens know this at the time but said as much to Maj. Gen. Hunter and Flag Officer Du Pont when he briefed them on May 1. He made it official when he submitted his plan in writing on May 17. As he told Hunter, he was going to allow Stevens to "make a dash at the railroad."

Given the go-ahead late on May 28, Stevens called for the 50th Pennsylvania, his allotted single regiment. He then augmented that on his own authority by adding detachments from the 79th New York and 8th Michigan, 80 troopers of the 1st Massachusetts Cavalry, and a section from the 1st Connecticut Light Artillery (commanded by the appropriately named Lt. John S. Cannon). Colonel Benjamin Christ of the 50th Pennsylvania would be in overall command of the raid.

Colonel Christ got his raiding party moving well before dawn on the morning of May 29, crossed at the Port Royal Ferry, the site of the New Year's Day battle, and proceeded inland toward the small village of Garden's Corner, not quite halfway to his goal. He advanced without his artillery, which seemed to have gotten lost and trailed about three hours behind the rest of the force, eventually catching up late in the day, too late to participate in the action but in time to help cover the withdrawal.

With the cavalry skirmishing ahead, Christ's force advanced cautiously, passed through Garden's Corner, and continued in the direction of Pocotaligo. "Save the driving in of the enemy's pickets several times, which caused us considerable delay," he reported, his men advanced steadily enough that the Federals were nearly in sight of the bridge they wished to burn by mid-morning. But that was about as close as they would come.

**Brig. Gen. A.R. Lawton commanded the Confederate troops in Georgia as part of General Pemberton's area of command.** (loc)

The Confederate resistance was sporadic but strong enough to slow down the Union column, forcing it to deploy into battle line several times. In the meantime, Rebel reinforcements advanced on Pocotaligo from McPhersonville, a few miles north of the railroad. Christ reported, based on information from a prisoner, that the Confederates opposing him numbered "at least 800."

The marshy ground around a narrow causeway delayed him as he approached Pocotaligo. The Confederate defenders had dismantled, but not destroyed, a small wooden bridge at the end of the causeway as they fell back, leaving only a few of the six-inch-wide stringers. Deploying his men to provide covering fire, Christ sent a company across on the slippery stringers. When this was accomplished and he had gotten the footboards of the bridge put back into place, he crossed over some 300 additional troops and engaged the Confederates for about two hours with the men on both sides fighting mostly from ditches in the marsh. Finally, with the day wearing on and his men running low on ammunition, Christ started to worry about the imminent arrival of Confederate reinforcements and ordered a withdrawal around 4:00 p.m.

Christ's concern was warranted. General Pemberton had received news of the Federal push toward Pocotaligo, and he responded quickly with orders to General Drayton in Hardeeville and to General A.R. Lawton in Savannah to send a regiment each with all possible urgency. "Hurry on your troops," he told Drayton in a clear demonstration of the importance of the railroad.

Many of the Confederates facing Christ's men were armed with shotguns, and Col. W. S. Walker, commanding them, insisted that he had only 76 men from a militia company called the Rutledge Mounted Riflemen and a portion of the "1st Cavalry Regiment, South Carolina," a militia organization under Maj. Joseph Morgan, opposing the much larger Union force. Nonetheless, several hundred reinforcements were headed for the area, though by the time they arrived and deployed, the Federals already had turned back. These reinforcements pursued the Yankee troops, following them at a distance all the way back to the Port Royal Ferry.

The return march challenged the Union foot soldiers, most of whom had been in motion since around 2:00 that morning. They had crossed the Coosaw, marched and skirmished their way to the causeway near Pocotaligo, struggled to get across the partly demolished bridge, re-laid the bridge planking, engaged the Confederates for about two hours, then marched back to their starting point "under a blazing sun" until they got some relief with the arrival of dusk. The Confederates let them march back largely unhindered, except for the Confederate cavalry firing on the Federal rear guard at Garden's Corner late in the evening. Most Union troops crossed the Coosaw by around 3:00 a.m., though stragglers continued to come in until around 5:00. All-in-all, these men had covered some 33 miles in 27 hours.

Casualties were light on both sides. The Union force lost two killed and nine wounded, while the Confederates lost two killed, six wounded, and one man missing.

Despite their exertions, the Federals had accomplished virtually nothing by their raid, though General Stevens said that "it was most successful as a reconnaissance or demonstration." He could not refrain from getting in a dig at General Benham by commenting that "it is very certain could the original programme have been carried out, that the whole line would have been broken up from Salkehatchie to Coosawhatchie."

All concerned seemed promptly to have forgotten the entire enterprise, especially since Maj. Gen. Hunter's army already had begun its move toward James Island. That occupied everyone's attention.

One might argue that the determined Confederate response to the half-hearted raid demonstrated the importance of the railroad and should have made it clear, even to General Benham, that Stevens' idea to destroy it had merit. Robert E. Lee's greatest fear was a major attack on the railroad. However, the Federals had other plans.

A portion of the plume once nodding over the traitors
of a soldier of the "Confederacy", of the First Regiment,
Carolina Volunteer Cavalry. It was taken from the Rebel
Island, in June 1862, in a fight between the Rebel horse
1st. Massachusetts Cavalry, by one of the Captains of the
him given to Brigade Surgeon Crispelb, who transmitted it
as a memorial of the advance upon Charleston.

# *The Navy Secures the Stono*

## CHAPTER FOUR

*MID TO LATE MAY 1862*

Thanks to Robert Smalls, Flag Officer Du Pont had a good idea of what to expect at the mouth of the Stono River. The batteries on Coles Island had been removed since Smalls had brought some of the guns with him, so Du Pont felt safe in assuming the ex-slave had been correct about the rest of the batteries along the river also having been dismantled.

Of course, he needed to confirm that, so on May 15, he wrote to Cmdr. John B. Marchand, commanding the blockading squadron off Charleston, recommending "a reconnaissance to be made by two or more gunboats" to investigate the information he had received from Smalls. At the same time, he also instructed the gunboat USS *Pembina* to report to Marchand for orders. Marchand wrote to Commander Parrott later that day, informing him that he (Marchand) would take the *Pembina* to Stono Inlet the next morning. That would leave Parrott once again in temporary command of the squadron, so Marchand instructed him to order the USS *Unadilla*, scheduled to arrive early that morning, to proceed to join the *Pembina* as soon as she did so. The USS *Ottawa* soon joined these two, and the three ships would scout and chart the Stono.

*Unadilla*, *Pembina*, and *Ottawa* were sister ships; identical, shallow-draft vessels of the *Unadilla* class of gunboats, 23 of which were constructed early in the war specifically to operate in the shallow waters of the southeastern coast. Known as "ninety-day gunboats,"

**"A portion of the plume once nodding over the traitorous brow of a soldier of the 'Confederacy,' of the First Regiment, South Carolina Volunteer Cavalry," captured by a member of the 1st Massachusetts cavalry on John's Island.** (lr)

**Union gunboats entered the Stono River in preparation for the landing of troops.** (loc)

each had been contracted to be built within that time frame. These 158-foot long, single-screw vessels displaced just under 700 tons, drew 9 feet, 6 inches of water, and were armed with an 11-inch Dahlgren smoothbore, two 24-pounder smoothbores, and two 20-pounder Parrott rifles. Prominent naval architect Samuel H. Pook designed these vessels, though he is better known for designing the City-class Mississippi River ironclads commonly known as "Pook turtles."

The navy spent the next few days locating and sounding the depth across the bar and trying to identify any obstacles. With 10-11 feet over the bar, the water ran deep enough for the gunboats to cross in a smooth sea, but the heavy swell made things tricky. If a ship caught a roller at its height, it would easily be carried across into the inlet. If not, it could be slammed down onto the bar, resulting in considerable damage or even loss of the vessel. Marchand exercised appropriate caution.

During these days of waiting for the right sea conditions, he kept the ships' boats busy sounding the inlet, dropping buoys, and sweeping for torpedoes, some 500 of which the Confederates had been reported to have placed. None were found.

**Cmdr. John D. Marchand commanded the Charleston blockading squadron under Flag Officer Du Pont and was responsible for preparing the Stono River for the arrival of Benham's troops.** (nhh)

About 9:00 a.m. on May 16, Marchand took his gig into the river to reconnoiter past the earthwork on Cole's Island known as the Palmetto Fort. After hearing that many, perhaps all, of the reported 48 guns in the area had been removed, he wanted to determine how many might still be in place. He used himself and his men as bait, but the Confederates did not fire on the gig as it approached. Marchand noted their flag flying above the fort along with "a small company of soldiers—among the last, an officer on horseback" watching him from the parapet.

He had to pass "within grape shot distance" of the fort and wrote that he "watched with much intensity for the flash of the cannon but none came," so he continued upriver "examining the deserted batteries."

The Confederates were not ignoring him completely, however. Once he had passed the fort,

a squad of soldiers—Marchand thought ten or twelve—who had moved upriver and hidden along the riverbank, ambushed his boat. He quickly withdrew, and, though the rebel soldiers continued firing on him, their poor marksmanship resulted in neither the boat nor anyone in it getting hit. As a result of this adventure, Commander Marchand determined that neither the Palmetto Fort nor its outworks would be serious obstacles when the Federals launched their attack.

On the 19th, he returned to the *James Adger*, leaving instructions with Acting Master Charles Boutelle, in command of the Coast Survey steamer *Bibb* and the ships' captains to take the three gunboats through the inlet and up to the junction of the Stono and Kiawah Rivers at "the first favorable moment without waiting for me." Conditions improved on May 20, so leading the way in the *Unadilla*, Boutelle brought the ships in. They anchored around 11:00, just about a mile below the village of Legareville on Johns Island, then waited for the squadron commander to join them.

**Alfred Waud sketched the *Unadilla* class gunboats.** (loc)

When they saw the approaching Federal gunboats two days earlier, the Confederates had burned most of the battery-related structures on Coles Island and at the Old Fort upriver on Battery Island. The Old Fort, so called because it had originally been built during the War of 1812 to deter the British, had been rebuilt and renamed Fort Pickens (not to be confused with the Fort Pickens near Pensacola, Florida). Still, most referred to it by its original name. The Union sailors celebrated the rising smoke and spreading flames as evidence that their enemies had retreated from their advanced positions along the river. This was, in fact, the case. Commander Marchand described the burning of "60 or 80" small buildings, mostly huts used to house the troops, as "a gloomy but magnificent sight in the bright light of the sun, had it been at night it would have been a splendid display."

Both Marchand, a Pennsylvanian, and the Maine-born Boutelle were highly experienced seamen. The former had been in the navy since becoming a

**Charles Boutelle, who surveyed and buoyed the Stono River in preparation for the James Island landings, later served eight years in the U.S. Congress as a Representative from Maine.** (msa)

midshipman in 1828. He had served in the East Indies and the Mediterranean and had seen combat in the Second Seminole War and the Mexican War. At the beginning of the Civil War, he took command of the USS *James Adger*, and Du Pont eventually assigned him to command the blockaders off Charleston. In 1864, aboard the USS *Lackawanna*, he participated in the battle of Mobile Bay.

Ironically, the *James Adger*, flagship of the Charleston Squadron, was named after a very prominent and successful antebellum Charleston businessman. From 1802 until his death in 1858, James Adger had been involved in cotton trading, banking, a variety of mercantile and agricultural enterprises, railroads, and shipping, in addition to serving in the state legislature and holding various city offices in Charleston. At one point, his many business enterprises reportedly made him the fourth richest man in the United States. Adger's Wharf on the Cooper River was named for him. His son, Capt. Joseph E. Adger served as Quartermaster of the 25th South Carolina Infantry.

Adger's namesake ship, a 1,150-ton sidewheel steamer, had been one of his packet vessels, part of a company he had founded in 1845 known as the "Adger Line." She had transported mail and cargoes on a regular run between Charleston and New York. Unfortunately for her, the vessel was docked in New York at the beginning of the war. The U.S. government seized her, turned her over to the navy, which converted her to a warship, and sent her back to help blockade her home port.

One member of the *Adger*'s crew when Marchand took command was a recently commissioned Naval Academy graduate named Alfred Thayer Mahan. He served under Marchand only briefly before transferring to another assignment, but Mahan would go on to a highly distinguished career as a historian and naval strategist. He is best known for his monumental work, *The Influence of Sea Power Upon History*, written some 25 years after the Civil War.

Acting Master Boutelle came from a seafaring family, and from age 15 spent most of his life either in the merchant service or as a volunteer officer (not a regular commissioned officer) in the navy, where he had gained a solid reputation "as a gentleman and meritorious person." In May 1862, he worked for the Coast Survey. One historian has referred to him as

USS *James Adger*, flagship of Charleston blockading squadron and named for former Charleston businessman, James Adger. (nhh)

"an almost unsung hero" because he "surveyed and marked all the major sounds and harbors along the South Atlantic seaboard," thus making fleet operations much safer and more effective.

Boutelle would be responsible for buoying the Stono River in preparation for the fleet that would land Hunter's army on James Island. Later in the war, he participated in the action against the ironclad CSS *Albemarle*. While commanding the USS *Nyanza* in August 1864, he received the official surrender of the Confederate fleet at Mobile Bay.

Around mid-afternoon on May 20, Commander Marchand joined what he oddly called his "holy-horrored squadron," and the gunboats moved cautiously upriver, randomly firing their 11-inch guns at suspected Confederate positions as they progressed. They passed the previously abandoned Legareville and the Old Fort, then approached the line of pilings that the Confederates had placed in the river as obstructions. Marchand inspected these and found a passage "50 feet wide and 4 ½ fathoms (27 feet) deep," more than enough for his gunboats to pass safely through so that he could explore further upriver. With that discovery, he decided to call it a day and ordered his ships to withdraw to the mouth of the river, where they would remain overnight. Boutelle ordered two buoys placed and planned to return the following day to finish the job.

Before allowing his ships to withdraw, Marchand did a very curious thing. "Before sunset," as he described it in his journal with no further explanation, "Captains Collins (*Unadilla*), Bankhead (*Pembina*), Creighton (*Ottawa*), and Boutelle (*Bibb*) with myself pulled in our boats and made a reconnaissance of the

Capt. Napoleon Collins commanded the USS *Unadilla* during the Secessionville campaign. He later went on to become a rear admiral. (loc)

Old Fort." He must have been extremely confident that the Confederates were gone, and fortunately for the Union Navy, he surmised correctly. The decision to have five ship captains, including the squadron commander, go ashore together merely to examine an abandoned earthwork may well have raised a few eyebrows and could have been disastrous. But, as things played out, the captains just looked around a bit, no disaster occurred, and they all safely returned to their respective commands.

Marchand's movements on May 20 prompted the Confederates to burn what they had not burned two days before and withdraw out of range of his guns as quickly as they could. The ships had a clear field of fire onto the main causeway from Battery Island, so the pickets from the 24th South Carolina, two companies under Lt. Col. Ellison Capers, took a roundabout route across a recently constructed footbridge which apparently could not be seen from the ships. They all escaped without injury, though one detachment panicked and threw its artillery piece into the pluff mud before retreating. Marchand wrote that the Confederate pickets "took to their heels and ran for their lives." Using the new footbridge, the Confederates managed to withdraw in an orderly way and thus escape. But they soon would return.

Later that evening, Col. C. H. Stevens, commanding the 24th South Carolina, sent some 60 men from Company E back to Battery Island, where they took up several positions near and inside the Old Fort. Six of them established an observation post in the magazine at the fort.

While exploring these ruins the following morning, two of the *Bibb*'s volunteer officers, John Bradford and Charles Boyd, almost literally stumbled over one of the Confederate soldiers hiding in the grass. The man was armed only with a bayonet, so Boyd's pistol convinced him to surrender. His comrades in the magazine soon came out as well, and the *Bibb*'s crew came up to help take these other prisoners.

As the crew took the six captured Confederates to the *Unadilla*, the *Ottawa*, covering the movement, spotted Confederate cavalry approaching and opened fire to keep the horsemen at bay. They also caused some "100 to 200 soldiers (to) rise and retreat to the pine grounds." Those men were the 60 or so who had been sent by Colonel Stevens the night before, though, whatever their number, they retreated before the power of the navy's big guns.

Distraught at the capture of the men, Stevens wrote to General Pemberton, "I beg to commend to your favorable consideration the men who were captured and, should an opportunity offer for exchange would be much gratified to have them returned to the regiment: Sergt. Samuel White, Corpl. Calvin Wilson, Privates Adam Carter, Charles Carter, B.C. Hutson, Andrew Hutson."

Following this excitement, Commander Marchand's ships continued upriver for about a mile to the "magnificent plantation belonging to a Mr. Paul Grimball . . . an old gentleman who seemed to be about 75 years of age." After going ashore to speak to Grimball, "who claimed to be a Union man," and exchanging recent northern newspapers with him for that day's Charleston papers, Marchand continued upriver to the plantation owned by Grimball's son, Thomas. At that point, Marchand determined that he need go no further upriver since he had found an extensive area of good, dry ground suitable for campsites upon which the Federals "might land legions for an attack upon the southern defense of Charleston."

This pleased Marchand since he knew he could maintain effective control of the Stono as far upriver as the Grimball plantations. Even so, he felt uneasy as he doubted whether or when the army would take advantage of the situation. "The gate is now invitingly open to the army," Marchand wrote in his journal, "and we only await their coming." Flag Officer Du Pont shared Marchand's doubts, believing that Maj. Gen. Hunter's men lacked spirit and depended too much on the intimidating presence of the gunboats. "Our troops will not fight," he wrote to his wife, "if gunboats are within their reach." He also had a low opinion of their character. "Our army here are depredators and freebooters," he wrote not long after the army had settled itself on Hilton Head. And, in fact, looting and a general lack of discipline were evident, which did not bode well for interservice cooperation or future success.

**Born in Connecticut, Clement Stevens came to South Carolina as a child and became one of Charleston's elite.** (scl)

# *The Confederates Dig In*

## CHAPTER FIVE

*SPRING 1862*

The remains of the fort today, located just south of the confluence of the Stono River and the Wappoo Cut, are completely overgrown and not open to the public. Several houses have been built on portions of the site. The fort was a 400 x 350-foot, five-sided structure that eventually mounted 20 guns. (jm)

When former First District commander Maj. Gen. John C. Pemberton replaced General Lee in overall command of the Department of South Carolina and Georgia (sometimes called the Department of South Carolina, Georgia, and East Florida), approximately 41,000 troops defended the department. About 35,000 of those were present and available for duty, the remainder being either untrained, unarmed, detached, or sick. Pemberton immediately began to reorganize the department while continuing to implement Lee's policy of defensive retrenchment. He quickly made one change, though: moving the departmental headquarters from Pocotaligo to Charleston.

He also ordered Brig. Gen. Ripley, commanding the Charleston district, to withdraw all the guns from the Coles Island fortifications and remove them to James Island. But he soon changed his mind about this when Governor Francis Pickens complained to Richmond about the move. Richmond—which is to say General Lee—did not order Pemberton to leave the guns in place. Lee merely reminded him of the importance of keeping the civilian authorities fully informed. Being no fool, Pemberton took the hint and left those guns where they were for the time being. They were not removed for nearly two months. Four of them were the guns taken by the *Planter*.

A Pennsylvanian by birth, Pemberton graduated from West Point in 1837—27th out of 50—and

**Governor Francis Pickens was a grandson of South Carolina's Revolutionary War hero, General Andrew Pickens, and a cousin of John C. Calhoun. Gov. Pickens took office on December 14, 1860, six days before South Carolina seceded, and served for two years.** (nps)

thus was a classmate of his Union opposite number, Henry Benham. Also part of that class were future Generals Jubal Early, Joseph Hooker, Braxton Bragg, and John Sedgwick. Pemberton sided with the Confederacy largely because of his Virginia-born wife, and he whole-heartedly threw himself into this new allegiance. Nonetheless, his northern birth made him an object of mistrust throughout the war, both in Charleston and, later, in Vicksburg.

Under Pemberton, when he took over were his district commanders—Col. Arthur Manigault, 1st District; Brig. Gen. Roswell Ripley, 2nd District (Charleston); Brig. Gen. Nathan "Shanks" Evans, 3rd District; and Brig. Gen. Maxcy Gregg, 4th and 5th Districts consolidated. This command stretched roughly 200 miles above Georgetown, South Carolina, southward to Savannah, Georgia. The districts and their commanders would be changed, combined, and rearranged several times during Pemberton's five months in command of the department.

Almost immediately, Pemberton found himself at odds with both his military subordinates and the civilian authorities in South Carolina. This started partly because he implemented General Lee's defensive plan, which required abandoning territory, something the civilian authorities, most of whom also were local landowners, did not like. Mostly, the Confederate government kept ordering him to send troops away from Charleston to reinforce what it considered to be locations under greater threat. For example, he was ordered to send a brigade of Tennesseans to Corinth, Mississippi, to make up for losses incurred in the battle of Shiloh. Later, he sent three South Carolina regiments to join the Army of Northern Virginia because of the threat posed by the landing of General McClellan's Army of the Potomac on the Peninsula.

Not surprisingly, Pemberton was especially unhappy about this last, ongoing requirement. He never knew when his forces might be weakened yet again, and he eventually sent away a total of eight regiments that previously had been deployed in the defense of his department. We can only imagine his consternation when he received General Lee's April 20 message informing him, not only would Lee "be obliged to reduce the force in your department," but that he had "no arms to send from here but pikes, which you might place in the hands of the men at the batteries, and give their guns to the troops in the field."

Whatever his feelings about pikes may have been, however, Pemberton dutifully ordered Brig. Gen. Gregg on April 22 to prepare to move north with the 12th, 13th, and 14th South Carolina Volunteer Infantry regiments. He replaced Gregg in command of the combined 4th and 5th Districts with Col. Peyton Colquitt of the 46th Georgia.

Having done this, he addressed an almost plaintive message to General Lee on April 23, stating that "in consequence of the removal of so large a part of the infantry force from this department, I have deemed it necessary to withdraw all troops except the cavalry between the Ashepoo and Oketie." The Oketie was a tributary of the Broad, and it entered that river from the west several miles north of Hilton Head Island. The Ashepoo flowed closer to Charleston, not quite halfway between that city and Savannah.

As a practical matter, Pemberton's withdrawal from this area meant conceding something like a third of the territory of his department—virtually everything between the Ashepoo River and the Georgia state line—and admitting that this move would leave the railroad "with no other protection than what the cavalry companies can afford, which is altogether insufficient." It was sheer good fortune for the Confederates that Generals Hunter and Benham, inexplicably it seems, had so little interest in the railroad.

\* \* \*

On April 15, 1862, per Maj. Gen. Pemberton's orders, Brig. Gen. States Rights Gist reported for duty to Brig. Gen. Ripley, who soon assigned him to the command of all Confederate forces on James Island. His name, "States Rights," might be seen as somewhat ironic given that he was born in a small village called "Union," located in the South Carolina back country, not far from Spartanburg. Gist's father, however, ardently supported John C. Calhoun during the Nullification years. When his son was born in 1831, as that crisis developed, the elder Gist named the boy in honor of his political views.

Gist was not a West Pointer but had been schooled at South Carolina College (now the University of South Carolina) and Harvard Law School. While engaged in his law practice, he also spent much of the 1850s in the

A cousin of Governor William Henry Gist, States Rights Gist became inspector general of South Carolina in 1860 and was responsible for preparing the state for war. (Tennessee State Library)

**Arthur Middleton Manigault was a descendant of a signer of the Declaration of Independence. He served with the Palmetto Regiment in Mexico and later commanded troops in several western theater battles during the Civil War.** (cmc)

state militia, eventually rising to the rank of brigadier general. Early in the war, he served as state adjutant and oversaw the mobilization of South Carolina's military forces. He served with Brig. Gen. Barnard Bee at First Manassas as a volunteer aide and was slightly wounded in that battle. Promoted to brigadier general in March 1862, he was assigned to duty under General Ripley the following month. He established his headquarters in the village of Secessionville. From mid-1863, Gist actively participated in the campaigns in the Western Theater until his death at the battle of Franklin on November 30, 1864.

Once in command on James Island, Brig. Gen. Gist stayed busy, making sure the construction of the defensive line proceeded. He oversaw the removal of artillery from Coles and Battery Islands and its reassignment to various positions within the new lines. He also withdrew the bulk of the 24th South Carolina from Coles Island, leaving only two companies nearby to quietly watch and report any Federal activity along the Stono. This was a result of the loss of the *Planter* and the increased Union movements in the area immediately thereafter.

It was those men who were driven away by fire from Federal gunboats on May 20, six of whom were captured the following day.

\*  \*  \*

In addition to his other concerns, Pemberton had continual problems with two of his more irascible brigadiers, Roswell Ripley and Nathan Evans. Each of those men had a reputation for being difficult with superior officers, very touchy about rank and prerogatives, and perhaps a little too fond of liquor.

Born in Ohio, Roswell Sabine Ripley had the same basic problem as his boss, Maj. Gen. Pemberton. He was a Yankee. As such, he never quite earned the complete trust of the southern people in his command, despite his marriage into two prominent South Carolina families. His wife, Alicia, was a Middleton and the niece of Ripley's fellow district commander, General Arthur Manigault.

Ripley was a West Point classmate of Ulysses S. Grant, both men graduating in 1843. His more studious habits allowed Ripley to finish 7th of 39 while Grant finished 21st in the class. He saw combat in Mexico, where he distinguished himself and was brevetted for gallantry at Cerro Gordo and

Chapultepec. Finishing the war as a brevet major, he was later posted to Fort Moultrie, South Carolina, where he met his future wife. After resigning from the army in 1853, he remained in Charleston.

Ripley also happened to be the nephew of Brig. Gen. James W. Ripley, who, as a captain, had commanded United States forces in the Charleston area (Fort Moultrie) during the 1832-33 Nullification Crisis and who served for the first two years of the Civil War as Chief of Ordnance of the Union army.

Nathan George Evans also was a West Point graduate, though just barely, finishing 36th of 38 in the Class of 1848. And he nearly was not admitted to the Academy at all. One "H. Williamson," who previously had been the nominee from that Congressional district, was deleted for unspecified reasons from the applicants' list for 1844, at which time Representative John Campbell recommended Evans in his place. Some sources state that Senator John C. Calhoun nominated Evans, but aside from the fact that Calhoun was not in the Senate at the time, the West Point admission records do not support that claim. Congressman Campbell submitted his recommendation letter for Evans on March 7, 1844, just over a month after the new cadet's 20th birthday. Evans was accepted on March 26 and reported to the Academy on July 1.

Nathan "Shanks" Evans was technically in command of Confederate forces on James Island the day before the battle of Secessionville. His actual participation was minimal. (loc)

He was known as "Shanks" because, according to his classmate and eventual Union General, John C. Tidball, he was knock-kneed. Evans missed the Mexican War but served on the frontier through the 1850s, eventually being promoted to captain of Company H of the elite Second U.S. Cavalry and earning the respect of his peers as an Indian fighter. When secession came, he sided with his home state. Commanding a small "demi-brigade" at First Manassas, he firmly held the Confederate left long enough for Thomas J. Jackson's troops to arrive and finally stop the Union advance. It could credibly be argued that Evans, rather than Jackson, should have been nicknamed "Stonewall" that day. Three months later, on October 21, his new, larger brigade in Leesburg, Virginia, the Seventh Brigade of the Confederate Army of the Potomac, defeated a Union force at the small battle of Ball's Bluff. When he returned home to South Carolina, Evans's star seemed to be on the rise.

**Brig. Gen. W. D. Smith was another of the general officers involved in the confusing Confederate command structure on James Island in the days before the battle.** (pb/ Virginia Historical Society)

Evans had proven to be better as a soldier than as a cadet. As a native South Carolinian, he had no difficulty being socially accepted. Indeed, he received a hero's welcome when he returned from his successes in Virginia to take command of the Third Military District on December 18, 1861.

\* \* \*

While the Federals readied to make their move onto James Island, the men in gray prepared to stop them. They could not prevent them from actually getting to the island—the U.S. Navy made that impossible—so the effort focused on creating a line of defense which would pin down the Yankees once they got there. This was why the smaller islands along the east bank of the Stono had been abandoned and their guns removed. All of this effort aligned with General Lee's and then Maj. Gen. Pemberton's defensive thinking, the only practical kind under the circumstances. It also minimized, though did not eliminate, the threat from the navy's big guns.

This defensive line was built under the overall direction of Brig. Gen. Ripley and the immediate direction of Brig. Gen. Gist, ran northwest to southeast along the approximate middle of James Island. The northern terminus, located just below the western end of the Wappoo Cut where it meets the Stono River, was a formidable earthwork eventually named Fort Pemberton. Amusingly, Ripley refused to call the fort by its actual name since he disliked Pemberton, and he always referred to it as the Wappoo or Elliott's Cut battery. With walls 12-15 feet high and 20 feet thick at the base, this heavily armed, bastioned earthwork went unchallenged by the Union forces throughout their stay on James Island, except for one brief exception.

Commander Marchand saw no need to challenge the fort or go further upriver than Thomas Grimball's plantation. However, Du Pont disagreed. Wanting to prepare for any eventuality which might result from the navy's cooperation with the army, and therefore wanting to ensure the control of the Stono as far up as the Wappoo Cut, he ordered Marchand on May 24, "to proceed with the gunboats and feel the battery" near there.

As events played out, Marchand could not "feel the battery" until May 29. The blockading squadron had a run of good luck during those five days, capturing or destroying several blockade runners. The disposal of the prizes took up much of Marchand's time. Moreover, the Confederates had a little surprise planned for the Federals on the Stono, a surprise they wanted very much to succeed.

*     *     *

The Confederates needed some success at that point, if only as a distraction from significant local problems. According to Governor Francis Pickens, there was "great disorganization" and "widespread dissensions," especially at Fort Sumter, though also among the other troops in the area. Tensions among the officers in and around Charleston ran high, and talk of a possible mutiny swirled among the men of the 1st South Carolina Artillery, who made up the garrison at Fort Sumter. Five of their number recently had deserted, spiked several guns before they left, and made their way out to the Union fleet. Several companies of troops in the area had been shifted around and reassigned to other posts, while knowledge of the recent mutiny at Fort Jackson, Louisiana, also had everyone on edge. The overall dissatisfaction among the Confederate troops at that time may be seen in the fact that, of the 7,209 troops reported by Brig. Gen. Ripley as being the "total present and absent" in late April, 398 were "in confinement," and another 124 were "absent without leave."

Colonel William R. Calhoun, nephew of John C. Calhoun and commanding officer of the 1st South Carolina Artillery, denied that there was a significant discipline problem with his men. Whatever that situation might have been, however, he was on bad terms with Brig. Gen. Ripley, as well as with his subordinates, Lt. Col. Thomas M. Wagner and Maj. Alfred M. Rhett, who also were on bad terms with each other. Ripley temporarily reassigned both Calhoun and Wagner, apparently just to get them away from each other for a while. The move also got Calhoun away from Rhett, who now commanded Fort Sumter as a result of the transfers.

It proved to be only a temporary respite. Later in the summer, after resigning from the army, Calhoun challenged Rhett to a duel, and, on September 15, Rhett killed him. In an obituary published in the Sacramento *Daily Union* on December 28, 1889, Rhett was described as "an exaggerated specimen of the Southern fire-eater," though that description might well have applied to Calhoun as well. Dueling was

Lt. Col. Thomas M. Wagner was a state senator and railroad executive before the war. He commanded a portion of the Confederate troops at the Tower Battery. He was killed in 1862 in an artillery accident. Battery Wagner on Morris Island was named for him. (scl)

legal in South Carolina and remained so until 1880. It was what gentlemen did to settle their disputes, so Rhett faced no serious repercussions, and he was said to have been one of General Ripley's favorites. Following a brief suspension from duty, Rhett was promoted to colonel and took Calhoun's old job as commanding officer of the regiment.

By that time, Lt. Col. Wagner also was dead, the tragic result of an artillery accident at Fort Moultrie on July 17. Among his other duties, Wagner had designed an impressive and formidable earthwork then under construction on Morris Island. At his death, that work became known as Battery Wagner. A year and a day later, on July 18, 1863, Battery Wagner became the site of one of the Charleston area's most famous Civil War battles, the unsuccessful assault by a Union brigade spearheaded by the black troops of the 54th Massachusetts Volunteer Infantry and later dramatized in the 1989 film *Glory*.

\*  \*  \*

The surprise on the Stono would be a Confederate ambush sprung on May 25. Pemberton planned to entice a Yankee gunboat or two far enough upriver to be reached by the guns of Fort Pemberton. The boats would be targeted as well by siege guns and field pieces quietly emplaced in the marsh grass on both sides of the river, plus whatever musketry could be brought to bear. The steamer *Marion*, with a smaller vessel in tow, acted as bait. The Confederates officially referred to the smaller vessel as a "gunboat" while the Federals more prosaically described it as "a large, flat hulk or floating battery." The *Marion* was to cross from the Ashley River to the Stono through the Wappo Cut, then proceed downriver to attract the attention of the Union gunboats.

Before she did this, another rebel steamer, the *Chesterfield*, was supposed to tow a "gunboat" of her own into what was hoped would be a disguised position in the marshes west of Secessionville and behind Dixon's Island.

Brigadier General "Shanks" Evans's forces also were supposed to be part of this ambush from positions on the west bank of the Stono. General Pemberton had told Evans of the impending attack on May 23 and instructed him "to have a battery of field artillery in readiness" to assist. He warned Evans, however, not to "get your artillery where you can't get it off." In the actual event, however, Evans was not involved.

If all went well, one or more Union ships would chase the *Marion*, be fired upon and forced to retreat, then hit hard in the flank by the hidden guns of the *Chesterfield*'s tow and the other artillery as they withdrew downriver. But all did not go well.

The *Unadilla* and *Pembina* made their daily run up the Stono on the morning of May 25 when they saw the *Marion* ahead and gave chase. However, to the Confederates' chagrin, they did not fully take the bait and pursue their quarry all the way to Fort Pemberton as the Confederates had hoped they would. In fact, they did not pursue the *Marion* very far at all as the *Chesterfield* was spotted as she attempted to drop off her charge. This spoiled the trap.

Johnson Hagood commanded Battery Wagner at the time of the unsuccessful July 1863 assault and later served from 1880-82 as governor of South Carolina. The football stadium at The Citadel is the Johnson Hagood Memorial Stadium. (loc)

When Union lookouts saw the *Chesterfield* and her tow just after the gunboats had passed through the gap in the obstructions below Grimball's, they opened fire and hit the *Chesterfield* once, causing her to withdraw with minor damage. *Pembina* then continued down river and left the rebel battery to the *Unadilla*, which anchored and opened fire again. This time, the *Unadilla*'s 11-inch, smoothbore shells fell somewhat short, but the Confederates surprised her by firing back with a heavy rifled gun. Captain Bonneau reported having hit the *Unadilla* twice. The shells actually missed, though they passed over the gunboat and, in doing so, apparently unnerved Commander Napoleon Collins, who immediately ordered his vessel to weigh anchor and move downriver out of range.

Colonel Johnson Hagood took note of the affair, lamenting that the "effort today of General Ripley to draw them within effective range of Fort Pemberton failed," but celebrating the "gallantry of Captain Frank Bonneau and of his men on our little floating battery." When the *Unadilla* withdrew, the *Chesterfield* returned and towed Bonneau's vessel to a position in the rear.

The ambush had not been successful even in damaging, much less destroying, a Yankee gunboat. But it was, perhaps, a small emotional victory for the Confederates to make the *Unadilla* flee in obvious haste.

\*  \*  \*

The Confederate defensive line continued southwestward from Fort Pemberton as a series of redoubts, artillery positions, and gun pits culminating in the Tower Battery on the Secessionville peninsula. Colonel Lewis Melvin Hatch designed and built this battery.

Hatch was yet another transplanted northerner. Born in Salem, New Hampshire, in 1815, he had lived and farmed near Charleston for more than 30 years before the war. He served as an aide to General Beauregard at First Manassas and then helped organize the 23rd South Carolina infantry.

Performing engineer duties in the spring of 1862, Colonel Hatch chose the site for the Tower Battery. Located on a "critically strategic piece of ground," it would become the bullseye for General Benham's attack on June 16. Events showed that its location was well-chosen. As historian Patrick Brennan has written, this battery "not only enfiladed the southern portion of the Confederate main defensive line but also provided access to a water route to the Confederate rear."

There were problems, however. Not everyone agreed with his choice of location. Hatch faced criticism for selecting that particular site and probably for the very reasons which Brennan noted. Its capture by Union troops would have rendered the rest of the Confederate line useless. Sitting at that location on the peninsula, the area behind it was a dead end.

Still, the criticisms, according to one supportive correspondent, were unfair; "the ill-conceived sneers of many," he called them. Writing in the Charleston *Mercury*, this anonymous supporter reminded Charlestonians following the battle of Secessionville that Hatch's forward thinking had contributed to the victory, and thus he deserved "the gratitude of the state."

The site was located on a dead end, though that was not an insurmountable problem. Hatch addressed the concern when he ordered the construction of a causeway from the tip of the Secessionville peninsula, not quite a mile behind the battery, northward across the water barrier of Clark Sound to a point near White House plantation, home of Ephraim M. Clark. Though narrow, "Hatch's Bridge," some three-quarters of a mile long, provided a shortcut that would (and, in the actual event, did) allow reinforcements to get to the Tower Battery in a timely fashion without having to rely on boats.

Ripley's defensive line would, in the end, prove an effective barrier during the one and only Union attempt to break it.

Building fortifications was all very well, but Ripley wanted a field command and lobbied hard to get one. He also, as previously indicated, was not on the best of terms with Maj. Gen. Pemberton. For one thing, he seems to have trusted no one's military judgment but his own. For another, he did not appreciate having so many of his troops taken from him for service elsewhere, though, obviously, Pemberton could not control that. Finally, he simply wanted to be in Virginia, where the action was.

Despite their personal antagonisms, Maj. Gen. Pemberton felt that Brig. Gen. Ripley's indispensable knowledge of the Charleston harbor defenses made him valuable, and he expressed this to General Lee. At about the same time, Governor Pickens encouraged Lee to replace not Ripley but Pemberton. Lee finally acknowledged, because of the swirling tensions around the two, that "one or the other must be removed." As a result, Ripley got what he wanted when he was ordered to Virginia on May 27. Pemberton replaced him in command of the Second District with Georgia Brig. Gen. Hugh Mercer (grandson of the Revolutionary War general of the same name).

Ripley arrived in Virginia in time to participate in the Seven Days fighting, where he commanded a mixed Georgia-North Carolina brigade in D. H. Hill's division. He stayed with the Army of Northern Virginia through all the campaigns of 1862 before returning to Charleston.

Mercer quickly found himself with a larger command as, on May 28, Pemberton reorganized his districts, combining the First and Second Districts into a new, larger First District under Mercer.

Hugh Mercer, a grandson of the Revolutionary War general of the same name, was expelled from West Point in 1826 for his participation in a boisterous party known as the "Eggnog Riot" but was pardoned by President John Quincy Adams and reinstated. (loc)

\*   \*   \*

Colonel Clement H. Stevens commanded the 24th South Carolina. A Charleston banker and railroad man with no formal military education, Stevens still had considerable military skill. He designed the ironclad battery constructed by the Confederates on Cummings Point (the end of Morris island opposite Fort Sumter). Stevens and Gist had been together at First Manassas as Stevens was the brother-in-law of General Barnard Bee and served on his staff. Indeed, he had been seriously wounded when Bee was killed

**Lt. Ellison Capers early in the war.** (scl)

at that battle. Stevens, himself, died during the Atlanta campaign in July 1864.

Along with his friend, Ellison Capers, Stevens organized the 24th South Carolina in April 1862. He became the regiment's colonel and Capers the lieutenant colonel.

Capers graduated first in the Class of 1857 at the Citadel and taught mathematics there prior to the war. The son of a Methodist minister, he became an Episcopalian minister, and eventually a bishop, following the war. Early in the war, he was the regimental major in the 1st Regiment South Carolina Rifles under Brig. Gen. Johnston Pettigrew but resigned that position in November 1861 to help Stevens organize the 24th South Carolina.

Like General Gist, he served in the Western Theater during the last half of the war. He replaced Gist as brigade commander when Gist was killed at Franklin. Capers was promoted to brigadier general shortly before the war ended.

The Confederates knew that Hunter would attack Charleston, and, as May moved toward June, they understood that the attack must come soon. Partly because of his concerns about a mutiny and partly because he seems finally to have accepted that the Federals wanted the cities instead of the railroad, General Lee wrote in a tone of near desperation to Maj. Gen. Pemberton on May 29:

> *The importance of defending both Charleston and Savannah to the last extremity, particularly Charleston, is earnestly brought to your attention. The loss of Charleston would cut us off almost entirely from communication with the rest of the world, and close the only channel through which we can expect to get supplies from abroad, now almost our only dependence. You will therefore make use of every means at your command to put these cities in the most perfect state of defense. . . . Let it be distinctly understood by everybody that Charleston and Savannah are to be defended to the last extremity. If the harbors are taken, the cities are to be fought street by street and house by house as long as we have a foot of ground to stand upon.*

**Capers as an Episcopalian bishop later in life.** (cm)

While Lee exaggerated when he said that Charleston was the only channel through which the Confederacy could receive aid, he did not stretch the truth much. The Union blockade, only a year old, was becoming more effective and less porous almost by the day, as clearly indicated by Commander Marchand's squadron's recent successes against blockade runners.

Governor Pickens understood and shared General Lee's sense of desperation. Two members of the Executive Council, William Porcher Miles and Andrew G. McGrath, wrote on the governor's behalf to General Pemberton on May 22, asking if he would object if they began making preparations for their own defense of the city should he be forced to withdraw his troops. They did not then know that Lee would order a "street by street and house by house" defense of the city.

Pemberton did not yet know that either. He responded that, while he hoped such a necessity would not arise, he understood that it might, so he appreciated their concern and would not object "provided the plans for defense are submitted to me and meet my approval." Understandably, he did not want any action they might take to interfere with his own defensive arrangements.

*   *   *

While General Gist dug in on James Island, Shanks Evans watched the flank. From his headquarters at Adams Run, some 30 miles west of Charleston, Evans spread his roughly 5,400 available troops across the mainland and on Wadmalaw and Johns Islands. This disposition allowed him to cover or at least observe the western and southwestern land and water approaches to the city.

The Union Army conceivably might have advanced along the railroad, though there was little actual danger of that given General Hunter's obvious lack of interest in it. More likely and fueling Evans' greater concern were three other possibilities, moving, in order, more or less west to east. First, Pemberton had to be concerned with a water approach up the South Edisto River, into the Edisto itself, and so to Willtown, from which a major road led east to the Ashley River and Charleston. Second, the Yankees had been occupying Edisto Island since February 12 and had pushed northward occasionally to Little Edisto and Jehossee Islands, forcing back Evans's pickets when they did so. Brigadier General Evans had just over 1,300 troops in that immediate area. A determined push by the Federals from there would very likely give them the Willtown Road. The third concern for the

Confederates was a move up the North Edisto River into the Wadmalaw River to Church Flats, from which the Federals could move directly east across Johns Island or again make a very short march north to the Willtown Road not far from the critically important Rantowles Bridge. The railroad itself ran only two miles from Church Flats.

Adams Run lay between the railroad to the north and the Willtown Road to the south, about five miles east of the Edisto River, thus putting Evans in a good position to move in any necessary direction in fairly short order. From there, he also would be able to fall back to protect the Rantowles Bridge, where it was crossed by the Willtown Road about halfway to Charleston. That is what Pemberton wanted him to do.

On April 11, Pemberton sent Evans a situation report, informing him that he had been obliged to weaken his department by sending four regiments northward to reinforce Confederate forces in Tennessee. Thus, Pemberton explained to Evans why he (Evans) needed to give up most of his artillery; all, said Pemberton, that was "not absolutely necessary" so that it could be added to "the defense of our interior lines of intrenchments" on James Island. He also ordered Evans to prepare to move all his troops in the direction of the Rantowles Bridge. Clearly, Pemberton was constricting and shortening his lines as he had been doing since he took command.

Evans responded the next day with a lengthy and somewhat tendentious account of his troop dispositions and an explanation of what he could do, if he could remain in place with his current troop dispositions, should the Federals advance. He implied that he should not have to obey Pemberton's order to consolidate around the Rantowles Bridge. Part of his response included a complicated plan involving his own and Brig. Gen. Ripley's troops, outlining what he foresaw as an envelopment of the Federal forces should they move on his positions. There was considerable wishful thinking involved in this since it depended on the Yankees going exactly where he wanted them to go and doing exactly what he wanted them to do, exactly when he wanted them to do it. Moreover, it required precise coordination between his troops and Ripley's.

Displeased, Pemberton responded with a terse note, instructing Evans to "make such a disposition of your force as to enable you to concentrate as suggested in my last letter to you."

General Evans kept active in patrolling his district and trying to respond to Union incursions. On April 29, he engaged the gunboats *E.B. Hale* and *Crusader,* which had moved up the South Edisto River to attack a Confederate battery at Pineberry or Grove Plantation. This was owned by John Berkley Grimball, one of the sons of Paul Grimball, whose plantation on the Stono would become part of the Union beach head prior to the battle of Secessionville.

The Union sailors destroyed the battery by driving off the defenders, then landing a party of men who spiked the guns and burned the carriages. Confederates directed by General Evans harassed the vessels, exchanging fire with them twice more as they withdrew following their raid. This engagement was just one of many such small actions involving Shanks Evans's men and the navy during this time period. It is noteworthy only for the modern reason that the Grove Plantation's main house remains open and in use today as part of the Ashepoo-Combahee-Edisto (ACE) Basin National Wildlife Refuge.

# *Establishing the Beach Head*

## CHAPTER SIX

*LATE MAY TO EARLY JUNE 1862*

The last two weeks of May, the period during which the Federal navy prepared the Stono River, were problematic for several reasons. The relationship between the army and navy soured quickly during the planning for the eventual assault on Charleston when inter-service cooperation was most important. Major General Hunter had created one of the most significant problems when he divided his department into three separate districts, charging Brig. Gen. Benham with the command of the largest of them, and simply leaving everything to Benham. Hunter "essentially removed himself from the communications loop. The result was chaos."

Historian Clayton R. Newell neatly summed up the problem, writing that Benham was "a better engineer than a line commander." This may be the reason that, in 1855, "perhaps understanding where his strengths lay," then-Captain Benham declined a promotion and transfer to major of infantry, remaining with the engineers. The war seems to have changed his mind about that.

On May 17, Du Pont addressed a seemingly small but more immediate and potentially quite serious problem when he wrote to Brig. Gen. Benham concerning proper protocol to be used between Navy and Army vessels. Du Pont wrote that he had just learned of an ugly incident between Lt. Alexander C. Rhind, commanding the USS *Crusader*, and the master, surnamed Cannon, of the Army transport

**From the Battery Island landing site looking southward, one can see the Atlantic Ocean four miles distant.** (jm)

The Battery Island Road, now called "Old Sol Legare Road," turned left here toward the causeway. The modern Sol Legare Road continuing past the turnoff did not exist during the war. The June 3 skirmish was fought in this area and to the left of the road. This also is the location of the July 16, 1863, fight that was the first combat by the 54th Massachusetts. (jm)

ship *Delaware* (not to be confused with the warship USS *Delaware* then serving in the North Atlantic Blockading Squadron).

Similar incidents had occurred previously, including one between the commander of another Army transport and Lieut. William T. Truxtun (grandson of Commodore Thomas Truxtun, one of America's earliest naval heroes), commanding the USS *Dale*.

As a matter of general security, navy vessels commonly stopped and boarded Army transports entering or leaving ports. According to Du Pont, the captain (or "master") of the transport, apparently objecting to being boarded, had been verbally abusive to Lieutenant Rhind and offered a "gratuitous insult" to him of such seriousness that the army's Brig. Gen. Horatio Wright had ordered the man's arrest. Du Pont noted that it "was not the first time that my officers

Fifth from right, next to Admiral David Porter, Commander Alexander C. Rhind commanded the ill-fated USS *Keokuk* in the ironclad attack of April 7, 1863, on forts Sumter and Moultrie. (loc)

have had to complain of such conduct" and expressed his hope to Benham that Master Cannon would be "discharged from the Government service."

Du Pont went on to assure Benham that he wanted nothing to interfere "with the harmony existing between the two services." With that in mind, he ordered all his ship captains no longer to board any Army transport "known to be such." He issued that "no boarding" order the very same day.

Brigadier General Benham never responded to Du Pont, but Maj. Gen. Hunter did. Writing to him on June 21, Hunter declared his complete agreement with Du Pont that the navy's blockading vessels, acting in effect as pickets, had a right and a duty to challenge and stop the transports if necessary. He expressed the hope that Du Pont would rescind his "no boarding" order so they could continue to do so. He condemned Master Cannon's behavior as being "in the highest degree reprehensible" and pledged to dismiss him from the service. He then immediately issued an order of his own, informing all transport captains that their vessels were subject to boarding by the navy's blockading ships and threatening prompt dismissal of any captain who did not comply.

Du Pont then addressed the Army commander, indicating his pleasure at Hunter's response. Perhaps growing conciliatory because of it, he asked Hunter, "as a favor," not to dismiss Cannon if the latter would recognize his error and apologize to Lieutenant Rhind. The record does not indicate whether Cannon ever did this. Rhind, in any case, went on to command the doomed USS *Keokuk* in the abortive ironclad attack of April 7, 1863, and eventually rose to the rank of rear admiral.

The Rivers Causeway no longer exists, and access is blocked from both ends. The distance from the northern approach to southern approach is approximately one-half mile across the marsh. This view is from the northern approach. (jm)

**View from landing site inland across James Island. Here, troops under General Isaac Stevens landed on June 2, 1862.** (jm)

However, even with that potentially explosive issue resolved, the question still loomed: how could the two services best cooperate to take Charleston? The same day Du Pont had written to Benham about protocol, May 17, Benham submitted a complex plan to Hunter regarding "the attack upon Charleston and the forts in that harbor." Two days later, Commander Marchand submitted a plan of his own to Du Pont.

The two plans were compatible, indeed nearly identical in their essential features, though there is no reason to believe that Benham and Marchand collaborated on them. The plans were compatible for the simple reason that taking and controlling James Island, and therefore Fort Johnson, was the obvious and most sensible move. That is why the Confederates worked so hard on their defensive line to prevent the Federals from succeeding.

Commander Marchand correctly stated in his plan that Fort Johnson was the key to Charleston since control of that fort meant effective control of the harbor. Union forces in Fort Johnson would have prevented any substantial water communication between Charleston on the one hand and Forts Sumter and Moultrie at the harbor entrance on the other, thus isolating them both, especially Sumter.

Fort Johnson sat less than a mile and a half from Fort Sumter, about two and a half miles from Fort Moultrie, the same distance from the Charleston Battery, and much closer to Castle Pinckney and Fort Ripley. Heavy rifled guns of efficient types unavailable to the Confederates, placed at Fort Johnson, would completely dominate the harbor. Moultrie still could be reached by a roundabout land route but on its own would have had no value. With Fort Johnson in Union hands, the Confederates would have had no choice but to abandon Sumter, Moultrie, and all the earthwork defenses on Sullivan's, James, and Morris Islands. Charleston Harbor would be open to the

Union forces, and Charleston itself must fall.

Commander Marchand called for the main assault force to land on James Island from ships in the Stono and then move directly against Fort Johnson. When he submitted this plan on May 19, the Confederates had not yet completed work on the James Island defensive line, and the idea, in any case, was fundamentally sound. He also called for a diversionary landing by Army troops at some point north of Charleston Harbor; perhaps Dewee's Inlet, some 10 miles away, or even Bull's Bay farther north. This force, advancing southward by land toward Mount Pleasant (across the Cooper River from Charleston),

Modern "Old Sol Legare Road" dead-ends approximately 100 yards ahead. This view is from the southern approach to the Rivers Causeway. (jm)

would hold any Confederates there or around Fort Moultrie firmly in place and prevent their moving to bolster the James Island line during the main attack.

General Benham's plan went into much more detailed terms for getting the assault force to James Island from their bases around Port Royal. Brigadier General Horatio Wright's division would be ferried as far as Edisto Island (part of it had been doing garrison duty on and around Edisto anyway), then march across Johns Island to the Stono. From there, it would cross to James Island in boats or on pontoons and link up with Brig. Gen. Stevens's division. That division, in the meantime, would make the entire trip by sea and disembark directly onto James Island. As with Marchand's plan, Benham's called for the attack across James Island toward Fort Johnson as the main assault. It also called for an Army landing around Dewee's (which he called "Dewey's") Inlet, but only after James Island had been secured.

The key element in both plans was the Army's all-out assault across James Island to take Fort Johnson. Because of the way events played out, however, this grand advance never took place.

At this point, problems arose because Brig. Gen. Benham believed that the navy was not pulling its weight and not following through on promises to support the Army. Moreover, he felt that the Army's own quartermaster general's office kept needed

From this location, General Stevens's troops began the campaign that led to the battle of Secessionville. (jm)

transport vessels from him. The latter was an internal army affair, but interservice cooperation was not. Had it been just a question of General Hunter and Flag Officer Du Pont working together, there probably would not have been a problem. But Hunter, perhaps not realizing what a loose cannon Benham could be, failed to keep him in check.

Captain Christopher R.P. Rodgers, Du Pont's second-in-command, met in person with Benham on Friday, May 16, to discuss Benham's overall transportation needs. Toward the end of that meeting, General Hunter arrived and informed the two men that he had decided to authorize the attack on Charleston, which they had been discussing for some weeks. He made this decision based on intelligence information about Confederate troop strength recently obtained from Robert Smalls. There were far fewer Confederates in and around Charleston than he or anyone else in the Union command structure previously had believed. Hunter's announcement changed the whole point of the meeting and prompted Benham to submit his detailed written plan to his commander the next day.

Before the meeting broke up, Rodgers suggested that Benham meet with Du Pont in person about his specific naval transportation needs for this campaign. Benham agreed, telling Rodgers and Hunter that he would go aboard the USS *Wabash* to meet with Du Pont the following morning, May 17. This was the very day on which Du Pont originally wrote to Benham about the problem with the navy's boarding of army transport vessels; the message to which Benham never replied but which finally was dealt with by Du Pont personally on June 21.

Benham did not show up for the May 17 meeting aboard the *Wabash*, nor did he send an explanatory message. A great deal of trouble and ill-feeling would have been averted had he done so. Most likely, he was busy working on his written plan for Hunter and perhaps distracted by that. However, Du Pont expected him. The flag officer waited all day on May 17 and through the morning of May 18 without hearing from General Benham.

Du Pont, quite understandably peeved, departed on his previously scheduled inspection tour around mid-day on May 18, leaving Rodgers in command at Port Royal. May 19 passed, still with no word from Benham. When Rodgers informed him that Du Pont had waited as long as he could but finally left, Benham got angry and began accusing the navy of withholding needed support from him.

He complained in apparently extraordinarily unpleasant language to Rodgers. Rodgers wrote a civil and constrained, but very detailed and unintimidated, explanation and rebuttal back to him on Thursday, May 22, reminding him of what had transpired at the May 16 meeting and of the fact that he had never come to consult with Du Pont as he had indicated he would. Rodgers pointedly told Benham that "any delay or inconvenience" was his own fault because of his "failure to explicitly make known to the flag-officer what assistance you wished for." He finished by saying that he thought Du Pont would return by Saturday, May 24 (which Du Pont did) and that transport vessels could be arranged then.

**Brig. Gen. Horatio Wright commanded one of the two Union divisions involved in the attack on Secessionville. As a major general, he later commanded the VI Corps of the Army of the Potomac.** (loc)

Secessionville historian Patrick Brennan correctly refers to what happened next as "a remarkable breach of protocol." Army General Benham went directly to navy Capt. John Goldsborough, farther down the navy chain of command and over whom he had no authority and tried to pressure him into taking action regarding the use of his ships for Benham's transportation needs. From this very uncomfortable position, Goldsborough diplomatically tried to assist Benham as he could while seeking the intervention of his superiors.

Goldsborough happened to be the younger brother of Flag Officer Louis Goldsborough, who commanded the North Atlantic Blockading Squadron. He obviously was under Du Pont and commanded a small blockading squadron around Wassaw Sound, just south of Savannah.

Upon his return on May 24, Du Pont learned about Benham's actions. Furious, he addressed himself directly to General Hunter. Writing from the *Wabash* that same day, Du Pont exercised remarkable restraint when he referred to Benham's correspondence with Rodgers by saying that "its tone and character are not such as should be addressed to an officer under my command." He went on clearly to imply that, while "I shall ever be ready to give you all the aid in my power," any further communication to him from the Army about the "important movements ... now in contemplation," should come from Hunter himself. DuPont had had enough of Benham. He later expressed his view in a letter to his wife when he wrote, "Benham is a great humbug."

It seems likely that this unpleasant incident helped make Hunter more conciliatory toward Du Pont when he later learned of the other unpleasant incidents involving the boarding protocols.

\*   \*   \*

General Benham gave the go-ahead for the troops to move on the evening of May 28. Brig. Gen. Stevens's truncated attack toward the railroad got started then as well. It was, in one historian's view, merely a "diversion," and Benham may well have thought of it as such himself. Either way, the rest of the Union forces began preparing to depart for their fateful James Island rendezvous.

Also on that day, Commander Marchand learned to his dismay that Flag Officer Du Pont had superseded him with regard to the Stono River operations in favor of concentrating on the Charleston blockade. Commander Percival Drayton in the USS *Pawnee* was ordered to take over command of the river operations.

Marchand declared that the decision was "mortifying" to him as these operations had become a kind of pet project of his and were closely integrated into the plan of attack which he previously had submitted to Du Pont. However, bringing Drayton aboard the *Ottawa* on the 29th, he explained the situation to him and steamed upriver far enough to examine Fort Pemberton. During that short excursion, the *Ottawa* followed a reported Confederate steamer to within sight of the fort and fired a few shells, which did no damage.

It took several days for the available transport steamers to be gathered, coaled, and arranged so that Maj. Gen. Hunter's troops, horses, supplies, and equipment could be loaded. Finally, all was ready, and the men of Brig. Gen. Stevens's division shoved off from Port Royal on the morning of June 2. Other than quite a few reported cases of seasickness, the trip proceeded without incident. By that afternoon,

**This is the view from the Battery Island landing site toward Ft. Pemberton, eight miles distant.** (jm)

Stevens's Yankee soldiers disembarked onto Battery Island.

General Wright's men had a much tougher time. They gradually had been shifting their camps eastward for a week or so. Largely in place on Edisto Island by June 1, they also started moving well before dawn on the morning of June 2. They first marched from their camps to the waterfront wharf, where they waited to be shuttled by boat the short distance to the landing on Seabrook Island. Some of them made that crossing in Robert Smalls' *Planter,* which had been detached for that service.

Major General Pemberton first thought that this landing heralded an attack on the railroad in the direction of Church Flats and the Rantowles Bridge to the northeast of Seabrook Island as the first step in a "general attack on Charleston." He said as much to Secretary of War George Randolph in two telegrams on June 3 and asked for reinforcements from North Carolina. That same day he ordered General Drayton at Hardeeville to have the 11th South Carolina move by rail to Adams Run and report to Shanks Evans. He also sent somewhat contradictory instructions to Evans at Adams Run. Evans received orders to defend his lines, protect the bridge, and also to attack the enemy at Legareville. In any case, Pemberton was wrong. The Yankees were not attacking the railroad.

From the landing, the Federals intended to march across Seabrook and Johns Islands along predetermined routes to Legareville, the small, abandoned village on the west bank of the Stono across from Battery Island. Since April, they had been using information provided by escaped slaves to study possible routes of march across Johns Island. Once at Legareville, Wright's men planned to cross the Stono to James Island and link up with Brig. Gen. Stevens. The straight-line distance from the Seabrook landing to Legareville was only about 15 miles. But the troops would not be marching in a straight line, and additional factors soon entered into the equation.

General Benham had allotted a single day for this march, but with delays piling up, it took the troops the better part of four days to make the trek. The weather caused most of the trouble. June 2 was one of the hottest days that most of the men could remember. Even before noon, the temperature reached 100 degrees, and the humidity approached 100 percent. Those men from Michigan, New York, Pennsylvania, and New England had never experienced anything like coastal South Carolina in the summer, and they wilted. Their heavy uniforms, draped with weapons and gear, could not have helped.

The men staggered along, discarding packs and blankets along the road. They fell out at such a rate that companies lost men by the score, and Company K of the 3rd New Hampshire counted only five men when it finally stopped for the day. Medics issued alcohol and quinine as stimulants, but this just made things worse. Unfortunately for the men, the supply train failed to keep up with the advance, which meant that food and water, especially water, became scarce. To make this miserable situation even worse, a boat had rammed into the wharf on Edisto Island, damaging it enough to seriously interrupt the flow of troops and supplies and causing even more delay, congestion, and confusion.

Mercifully, General Wright finally ordered a halt to the march that afternoon, allowing his troops to rest and regroup. The men generally just lay where they stopped, exhausted and largely without food or water, scattered along the roads on Johns Island through the night of June 2. The next morning, it started to rain.

The rain fell hard, accompanied by severe winds, and continued almost without pause for the better part of 24 hours. The men had little food or shelter, and water was limited to whatever rainwater they could collect. Wright ordered everyone to hold in place so that he could affect repairs on the Edisto wharf and allow time for the stragglers to come up. During the day, many men foraged on their own for food. Shank Evans' cavalry dashed in for some minor harassment,

This view shows the turnoff from former Battery Island Road (modern Sol Legare Road). The dirt approach is now called Old Sol Legare Road. (jm)

but no serious fighting occurred. The weather and the "indifferently armed" Rebel horsemen both contributed to that.

Among other problems, General Wright had ordered the destruction of all bridges once the division had crossed them. One of them, however, was burned with half of the troops still on the wrong side. Those unlucky soldiers had to wade across the shoulder deep water, carrying their gear above their heads. This slowed down their movements even further and resulted in the loss of much ammunition.

On June 4, the rain stopped, and at least some rations finally arrived and were distributed. General Wright ordered a review of his troops. This was less for pomp and show and more to let the officers and NCOs put their units back into proper order. Predictably, the review quickly became something of a mud march as the men moved along the soaked and sometimes flooded roads, but it accomplished its purpose. The division resumed its advance toward Legareville that evening. The men marched all night, part of the time in a renewed rainstorm which began around 2:00 a.m. and did not let up until the following afternoon. They finally began arriving at their destination around 8:00 a.m. on June 5, with exhausted troops straggling in throughout the day.

Had the Confederates managed to organize any sort of coherent attack on the strung-out Union troops on June 3–4, the Federal advance on Charleston would have collapsed right then. Shanks Evans received some criticism for staying stationary, but the rain bogged down his men, just as it slowed the Yanks. Moreover, they were waiting for the Union attack, which Pemberton had told Evans was coming his way.

By the time Wright's division had slogged its way across Johns Island to Legareville, Stevens's men already had seen the elephant.

# THE CIVIL WAR BATTLE OF SOL-LEGARE ISLAND
## JULY 16, 1863

### IN HONOR OF
### THE MASSACHUSETTS 54th REGIMENT

During the Civil War (1861-1865) Sol-Legare Island was the site of several camps, artillery positions and battles. On this date, one of America's first African American Army Regiments, organized in the North and led by Union Gen. Alfred Terry; bravely gave their lives to win the freedom of enslaved Africans who were held in bondage here and on plantations throughout the south. 5,200 Federal Troops occupied this Island. The 54th waged a gallant battle but lost 14 men. 17 were wounded and 12 missing. It is with great pride and humble gratitude that we honor their unwavering courage and sacrifice for a moral cause.

ERECTED BY ISLAND HERITAGE FOUNDATION
AND FIELDING HOME FOR FUNERALS
### 2006

# The Day of Trial Is Upon Us

## CHAPTER SEVEN

### *EARLY JUNE 1862*

At the end of May 1862, Confederate forces on James Island available to oppose the Union landing force numbered only 3,925 men, listed as "aggregate present." By pulling in additional troops from surrounding areas, Maj. Gen. Pemberton had increased that number to about 6,500 by mid-June. Nonetheless, he was worried, as was Robert Barnwell Rhett, owner of the Charleston *Mercury*. In an apparent effort to raise the spirits of Charlestonians, remind them of the efforts of their forebears, and energize them for the coming struggle, Rhett published a lengthy, detailed, and nearly day-by-day account of the earlier British siege of Charleston in 1780.

Noting the Union landings on James Island and the presence of numerous gunboats in the Stono River, Rhett introduced his historical piece by writing, "it seems that the attack on Charleston is imminent . . . and that the day of trial is upon us."

Whatever Rhett's thinking, the entire Confederate high command clearly focused on how to stop what looked more and more like a juggernaut. With Army of the Potomac commander Maj. Gen. George McClellan all but knocking on the gates of Richmond, Gen. Lee's almost panicky May 29 letter to Maj. Gen. Pemberton about defending Charleston to the last ditch illustrates this concern quite clearly. As June progressed, Richmond continued to call on Pemberton for more troops which he simply did not have to spare. At that point, the total force he had

**Visitors tracing the Secessionville campaign will also see memorialization of later Federal efforts.** (jm)

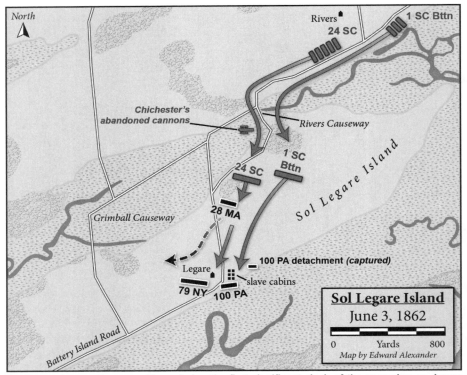

**SOL LEGARE ISLAND**—Troop positions during the first significant clash of the campaign on James Island. Coincidentally, this is the same ground on which the first fighting by the 54th Massachusetts took place just over a year later.

available for the defense of the entire Charleston area numbered no more than 10,000 men, roughly the equivalent of a single division in McClellan's army, though just about equal to the total available force in Hunter's. All things considered, the situation did not look good for Charleston or the Confederacy.

Northerners, on the other hand, felt quite confident. As one editorialist opined: "Doom hangs over wicked Charleston. That viper's nest and breeding place of rebellion is, ere this time, invested by Union Arms—perhaps already in our hands." That, of course, proved to be overly optimistic, but given what information civilians received at the time, the optimism was understandable. Not all northerners shared it, though. Commodore Du Pont wrote to his wife on June 13 that "the army operations I think have been a dead failure—Drayton thinks it highly probable they will meet with some disaster."

**Commanding the Gist Guard, South Carolina Heavy Artillery, Capt. Charles Edward Chichester had the bad luck to lose three of his four carronades in the marsh near the site of the June 3 skirmishing.** (cmc)

He could not have known how quickly Commander Drayton would be proven right.

\* \* \*

The names of famous local units hold a familiar place in Civil War Charleston's history: the Charleston Battalion, the Eutaw Battalion, and the Palmetto Guard, for example. The Gist Guards, though somewhat lesser known, still played an important role in these unfolding events.

On the evening of June 1, Capt. Charles Edward Chichester, along with some 70 members of the South Carolina Heavy Artillery company known as the Gist Guards made their way toward Sol Legare Island. He intended to deploy four 42-pounder carronades in a previously built earthwork near Legare's Point. The Confederate artillerymen planned to fire on any unsuspecting Union ships which might come into range the following day. Unfortunately for him, Chichester's timing and his luck both turned out to be very bad.

Carronades were short, relatively light-weight cannons compared to standard artillery pieces of the same bore size. A 42-pounder gun (that is, a cannon firing a 42-pound solid shot) weighed around 9,000 pounds, three times the weight of a 42-pounder carronade. This was largely because of the much shorter barrel length of the carronade (71 inches versus 129 inches). Too big and heavy to be truly mobile, the standard 42-pounders were designed to be placed in fixed fortifications. Carronades, on the other hand, though heavy for field guns (the famed 12-pounder "Napoleon" only weighed 1,200 pounds), could be moved around as needed, as Chichester was doing.

Called "carronades" because they first were manufactured at the Carron Iron Works in Scotland, these pieces essentially were artillery versions of large-bore sawed-off shotguns and were extremely destructive at close range. The British referred to them as "smashers." The disadvantage of their short range made them vulnerable to an enemy who could sit off with longer-range guns and fire at the carronades with no risk of return fire. The Confederates in Charleston had quite a few carronades in their artillery inventory. Of the four in Chichester's battery, he would lose three.

Around 10:00 p.m., the Confederate column slowly advanced toward Sol Legare Island, crossing the marsh on the Rivers Causeway, so called because it led to the Rivers house not far from Secessionville. Eight horses pulled each of the heavy carronades; the usual team for a field piece was either four or six horses. Though necessary, the additional horses made the teams and the loads somewhat unwieldy and harder than usual to manage. Unhappily, the gun crew lost control of one of the 3,000-pound carronades, which slid off the side of the narrow causeway and buried itself and its carriage in the pluff mud. The men labored hard but were unable to retrieve the heavy, awkward piece. They ultimately left it, pushing some timbers under it for support and intending to come back for it later. They still had the three other pieces which they needed to get into position before dawn.

The next morning, June 2, sometime around 10 a.m., Chichester's exhausted men were asleep around their guns when they and another Confederate battery closer to Secessionville came under fire from the USS *Ellen* and USS *E.B. Hale*. The vessels fired from positions not in the Stono River but to the south in the Folly River. Most of the *Ellen*'s 52 shots were aimed at Secessionville itself and the nearby battery, with little effect except the wounding or killing (accounts differ) of a horse. The *Hale*, however, had briefly run aground well behind the *Ellen* and, being within Chichester's range, exchanged a few shots with the Confederate battery. She withdrew downriver apparently to replenish her ammunition, then returned and resumed the exchange. Chichester probably did not fire at the *Ellen* because of the limited range of his guns though he fired some 70 rounds at the *Hale*, apparently, and indeed astonishingly given the range, doing little or no damage.

Commander Drayton reported that, despite being under fire for about an hour and seeing the Confederate projectiles "landing within a few yards at times," his ships were "untouched." Likewise, Chichester's battery suffered no harm. "No casualties occurred except a few scratches from splintered trees and fragments of shells." It seems that neither side had reason to be proud of its marksmanship during this encounter.

Commander Marchand heard this lengthy exchange of fire and became concerned that it meant a Confederate attack on his gunboats. He signaled the

Sketch of gunboat USS *E.B. Hale*, foreground, which later served as part of the Charleston blockading fleet and engaged in river activities in the Charleston area. (loc)

USS *Flambeau* to get closer and determine whether the vessels needed additional help. Finally deciding they did not, Marchand withdrew the *Flambeau* about the same time he saw several transports coming up from the direction of Port Royal and entering the Stono Inlet. These, he noted in his journal, were the ships which "landed our army under General Benham for the purpose of attacking Charleston."

Oddly enough, and despite having been spotted by the two Union vessels whose captains seem not to have communicated this information to the army, Chichester's men and guns remained completely undiscovered throughout the afternoon and evening. Meanwhile, the Union infantrymen from Brig. Gen. Isaac Stevens's division began landing on Battery Island and moving toward Sol Legare around 3 p.m. According to an anonymously written newspaper report, "the enemy and a small party of our men lay near each other all night at Legare's."

\*   \*   \*

At 3:00 p.m. on June 2, 1861, the 79th New York Volunteer Infantry, known as the "Highlanders," formed ranks at their headquarters in New York City and marched off to war. One year to the day and the very hour later, at 3:00 p.m. on June 2, 1862, those same men disembarked from their transport vessel onto Battery Island led by their commander, Lt. Col. David Morrison. They were the first Union troops to land in what was hoped would be the grand assault on Charleston.

An anonymous soldier from the 100th Pennsylvania ("Roundheads"), who signed himself only as "C," claimed in a June 7 letter to the Wheeling

*Daily Intelligencer* that his unit, not the New York regiment, had been the first to land. "On Monday evening" (June 2), he wrote, "we landed per gunboat *Hale* at Old Battery, the first troops to the assault." He claimed that honor for the regiment's Company A, though he seems to have been unaware that the Highlanders already had been on the ground for several hours. It appeared that the *Hale* moved on to transport duty following her exchange with the Gist Guard.

Almost immediately after coming ashore, Col. Morrison pushed a company forward to reconnoiter the small island and take a preliminary look at neighboring Sol Legare Island. The Yanks would have to traverse Sol Legare before they could cross to the larger James Island, where they knew Confederate defenses waited.

Morrison chose his Company E to make this preliminary reconnaissance. That company had been his own before his promotion to the command of the regiment. On June 2, Capt. William St. George Elliot, the son of the regiment's original commanding officer, commanded Company E. The younger Elliott cautiously advanced across Sol Legare almost to the causeway but saw no Confederates until a few pickets on James Island showed themselves. The Yanks and Rebs took stock of each other but did not open fire though, at some point later, an officer on General Gist's staff, Capt. Carlos Tracy, and then Gist himself, did draw fire as they observed the Union troops from across the marsh. The Federals then withdrew some distance, made camp for the night, and prepared to do battle with the swarms of mosquitoes that lay in wait for them in their marshy campsites.

Commodore Du Pont reported that Commander Drayton, who was there, had a decidedly negative view of the landing, believing that there "seemed no plan, no arrangements . . . things looked to him as if (the soldiers) would very soon be driven back to the vicinity of the gunboats."

\*    \*    \*

During the evening, Capt. Chichester quietly began moving his guns to safety, trying not to draw attention to his artillerymen. Somehow, he got past Captain Elliott's pickets and onto the causeway. His luck there, however, was no better than it had been the previous day. Despite moving slowly and cautiously, he lost two more of his carronades when they slid off the causeway and into the mud not far from where the first one had been lost. Again, his men labored unsuccessfully through the night to retrieve them, and again they had to leave the guns behind at daybreak. The Confederates, however, would try to get them back.

There was a brief ruckus in the early morning hours of June 3, which has been described differently by witnesses from the two sides. The 79th New York's regimental historian, William Todd, wrote about a Confederate cavalry patrol inadvertently stumbling into the New Yorkers' camp, probably just feeling for the enemy and unsure how far the Yanks had fallen back. According to Todd, the horsemen got away in the darkness and the ensuing noise, confusion, and shooting, though not without suffering at least one casualty. He noted that the following morning when it was light enough to see, the New Yorkers found "a cap clotted with blood and a cavalry sabre lying near it."

The Confederates, on the other hand, explained this short encounter as an ambush by "a party of the villains" on a squad of scouts, some 20 or so men from the 24th South Carolina. The approximate timing and location of the incident are the same in both accounts. Whichever of them most accurately described what happened, both sides agreed that little damage was done.

What then happened on June 3, the first serious ground encounter between Rebs and Yanks in the area was the unintended result of the loss of Chichester's three guns. The Federals would not have known about the abandoned guns until later in the morning when it got light enough to see. The Confederates knew they had been lost and wanted them back, so General Gist gave the job to Lt. Col. Ellison Capers of the 24th South Carolina.

Shortly before dawn, Lt. Col. Capers mustered his men and set out from their camp near the Rivers house, roughly half a mile west of the Tower Battery at Secessionville, at the point where the lower section of the Battery Island Road (known today as Old Military Road), makes a sharp westward turn as it approaches the northern end of the Rivers Causeway. Moving forward with Companies A, B, D, and E from his regiment to retrieve the lost guns, he quickly realized that he first would have to push the Union pickets away from the causeway to accomplish that mission.

Two companies of pickets, neither from his regiment, already watched near the causeway when he arrived on the scene, so he incorporated them into his force. They were the Charleston Riflemen (Company A) of Colonel Gaillard's Charleston Battalion and the Beauregard Light Infantry (Company E) of Colonel Simonton's Eutaw Battalion. They had, Capers wrote, been "driven in, and the enemy's advance (was) just behind our guns," that is, in position on or near the southern end of the causeway apparently within sight of Chichester's three lost carronades.

The Union troops facing Capers's men were a detachment from the 28th Massachusetts, the "Faugh a Ballagh" or "Clear the Way" regiment which later would become part of the famed Irish Brigade. At this point, the regiment formed part of the First Brigade of Brig. Gen. Isaac Stevens's division and Lt. Col. MacLelland Moore commanded it.

The Irishmen joined Capt. Elliot of the 79th New York as part of a combined picket force. Elliot had led the previous afternoon's reconnaissance and then had withdrawn a short distance west of the Legare house back in the direction of the main Federal body for the evening. His men skirmished in the brief flare-up earlier in the morning. The combined force consisted of Elliot's New Yorkers, two companies from the 28th Massachusetts, and some 160 men from the 100th Pennsylvania.

Elliot ordered the troops eastward as far as the Legare house, then sent the Irishmen northward up that part of the Battery Island Road, which led to the causeway. The rest of the men occupied Legare's main house and several slave cabins just to the east and the fields directly in front of them, no doubt curious and concerned about what their Massachusetts comrades would stir up. They would find out soon enough.

The Irishmen disappeared into a tree line perhaps a long quarter-mile in front of Legare's, passed through the woods and may have exchanged a few shots with the Confederate pickets just before Colonel Capers's arrival with the 24th South Carolina. Shortly thereafter, Capers attacked, first sending the Marion Rifles (Company A) of his regiment forward as skirmishers, then following up with his other five companies.

The Union troops in the rear could hear a growing volume of fire and then saw the 28th Massachusetts come tumbling out of the woods in considerable disorder, a few men at a time. The New Yorkers and Pennsylvanians formed a line of battle and waited. Captain James Harvey Cline of the Roundheads criticized the Irishmen's performance, later writing that the 28th Massachusetts "broke and ran (at) the first fire they received," though that was an exaggeration. Cline himself soon would become a prisoner.

Capers pushed his men forward to the woods and, shortly thereafter, through them. He then halted his troops and had them take cover just inside the tree line facing the Federals across the open field. There his men and the Yanks exchanged fire for some three-quarters of an hour. Capers described the Federal fire as "severe" but noted that most of it was high and passed over the heads of his men, a situation not untypical of inexperienced troops.

He finally decided to assault the Federals across the field but delayed this movement briefly when Col. Gaillard arrived with the rest of his battalion. Grateful for the reinforcements, he directed Gaillard to take position on his left. Then, rather conspicuously on horseback, Capers led a mixed force of several companies, his and Gaillard's, forward across the field in a determined push toward the Legare house.

Shortly before this, some of the Roundheads had moved to their right and strengthened the force around the slave cabins. Unfortunately for them, this produced a gap in the Union line, which Capers saw and successfully exploited.

The Federal skirmishers grudgingly fell back toward the main line around the house and cabins. Some of the Yanks retreated westward back toward their landing site, thus enabling the Confederate advance, specifically Company C, the "Irish Volunteers" of the Charleston Battalion, to cut off and capture Captain Cline and some 20 other Roundheads in the area around the slave cabins. The Confederate right, exposed and in the open around the Legare house at that point, came under fire from the Union gunboats. With that, Capers gathered his prisoners and ordered his force to retire. Both the *Mercury* and the *Courier* of June 4 reported the fighting and the arrival of the prisoners.

Parenthetically, on this same ground, just over a year later, that the 54th Massachusetts received its baptism of fire. A historical marker on the site today notes the later action.

The Confederates marched their captured prisoners to Fort Johnson. There, they were loaded aboard the seemingly ubiquitous *Etiwan* for transport to Charleston in the charge of a detachment of artillerymen from Col. Thomas Lamar's battalion. On arrival, they marched to the city jail under the less than friendly gaze of the locals and were handed over to John T. Milligan, the chief jailor. Eventually, they were moved to a prison in Columbia, where they remained for several months. Late in the year, following transport to Annapolis, Maryland, they were exchanged.

Near the Legare House, the fire of the Union gunboats proved to be accurate, thanks in large measure to one instance of effective army-navy cooperation. army signal officers, Lieut. Ocran H. Howard and Lieut. Edward J. Keenan worked with the navy to coordinate indirect fire from the ships' guns to the area around the structures. Howard stayed aboard the *Unadilla* while Keenan positioned himself forward so that he could see both the ship and the Union troops involved in the fighting. Keenan's signals to Howard and Howard's to the ship's gunners effectively coordinated the vessel's fire support that day and on a number of other occasions over the ensuing two weeks.

In the end, the June 3 fighting might fairly be called a draw. The Confederates got the best of the skirmish itself but abandoned the field and failed to accomplish their actual mission, which had been to retrieve Chichester's guns.

*    *    *

As so often happened after a battle, it soon began to rain. For several hours, the Union troops remained in place and watched the Legare fields and woods through the downpour in case the Confederates should attack again. But Capers had withdrawn, and the hard rain kept the Confederates' heads down. The *Mercury* reported that "from nine o'clock in the morning until late at night the rain poured down in continuous showers." Brennan writes that the rain, in fact, did not begin until after the Confederates had withdrawn, closer to 11:00. Either way, what happened later in the day took place in the middle of a storm. During these same rainy days, Brig. Gen. Wright's men were still slogging their way across Johns Island. Indeed, from

June 3–10, it seems to have rained, often quite heavily, nearly every day.

Around 3:00 p.m., a detachment of the New Yorkers cautiously advanced to reconnoiter. They discovered the three half-buried carronades and one of their wounded comrades, Pvt. Benjamin Clarke of Company G, "almost dead from loss of blood."

"Two of the guns were found to be in good order with ropes attached," so the men went to work and hauled them out of the marsh. Putting their wounded friend onto one of the carriages, they brought him back to camp as well. The third gun proved resistant to their efforts due to a broken wheel, so they eventually returned to camp with only two trophies. The unfortunate Private Clarke died the following morning.

Much of this work took place under fire since the Confederates apparently thought the enemy was preparing to attack across the causeway. Part of the Eutaw Battalion came up to support the Preston Light Battery (Co. A, First South Carolina Artillery). These forces exchanged fire with the 1st Connecticut Artillery until the Union troops fell back with their two captured carronades. A patrolling detachment from the 8th Michigan retrieved the third gun on the following day.

What ultimately happened to those three guns is unclear. According to one Reb who explored the abandoned Union camps in early July, "one of Chichester's guns has been left behind." If so, it mostly likely had been spiked or otherwise disabled.

Despite the prisoners taken on June 3, the fighting editors of the Charleston *Mercury* were displeased with the outcome of that day's skirmish. Understanding the threat from the Union Navy's guns, they declared that Confederate policy should always be "to attack at once and furiously. Gunboats cannot fire upon their own men, if ours get close up. . . . Ball's Bluff and Jackson's fight with Milroy should be our models."

Considering the typical relationship between Civil War generals and newspapermen, one can only wonder how General Pemberton received that advice.

# Does It Ever Get Dry in This Country?

## CHAPTER EIGHT

### EARLY JUNE 1862

Anticipation, preparation, false alarms, and rain—lots of rain—filled the next few days.

A New York soldier described "the wind blowing a gale and the rain coming down in torrents." Colonel Hagood reported that one of his pickets was asked by "a half-drowned Yankee" picket, "I say, does it ever get dry in this country?" Commodore Du Pont wrote to his wife that ships dragged their anchors and "for June, it seemed quite a violent gale." One Connecticut boy wrote on June 19, "I have not had a d----d rag of dry clothing on me for the last two weeks." A Confederate soldier described the rainstorms of those days as "a perfect deluge of water. The roads are terribly boggy and muddy, and the earth like so much slush." A Union artilleryman wrote of the soggy campsites saying, "We lay nights between the cotton rows, sometimes only our heads out of water." One of the 79th New York Highlanders wrote, "Whew! How sour and mouldy everything about our tents smelled."

Just as the northern boys had never experienced southern heat before, they also had never experienced southern rain. Perhaps a New Hampshire infantryman summed it best when he wrote, "The rains descended, and the floods came, and it really seemed as if it had never rained before. . . . No one except the initiated can understand how fast the rain falls at the South in a violent storm."

Given these conditions, though his men certainly were "initiated," it is hard not to feel some sympathy

**This view looks south from Artillery Crossroads toward the battlefield.** (jm)

**This view looks west from Artillery Crossroads toward the Confederate position at the Presbyterian Church.** (jm)

for Shanks Evans, who has been criticized both by his contemporaries and by historians for not being aggressive enough. Secessionville's primary modern chronicler, Patrick Brennan, wrote that Evans "was letting one of the truly golden opportunities of the campaign slip from his grasp" and, in the end, could do no more than report that he was "unable to ascertain the exact intentions or design of the enemy." While this may be true, it also should be remembered that Evans's men on Johns Island dealt with the same intense and near continuous rain which had General Wright's Union troops thoroughly bogged down.

Whatever has been said about Evans's failure to engage the enemy during those days despite the fact that Rebs and Yanks lay only a few miles apart, the horrible weather conditions offer at least a partial explanation and ought to be taken into account. General Mercer even reminded his men to rely on their bayonets if the rain fouled their muskets. Or perhaps this all simply should be viewed as a demonstration that God, as the Gospel of Matthew tells us and one of the Highlanders joked about, "raineth upon the just and the unjust." The New York soldier spoke of "unjust Johnnies" and "just Yankees." The reader will decide which was which, but it most certainly did raineth hard and indiscriminately upon everyone in the Charleston area for a solid week. The weather affected the operations of both armies.

There was much communication on June 3-4 between Maj. Gen. Pemberton and President Davis on the one hand, and Pemberton and Evans on the other. Davis wanted troops to reinforce the Richmond defenses. Pemberton expressed reluctant willingness to send them, but clearly, Charleston was going to take a back seat to Richmond at that time, despite General Lee's earlier concerns. Pemberton and Evans discussed attacking Wright's Federal line, which stretched out between the initial landing point and Legareville on the eastern side of Johns Island. However, as events played out, after all the telegrams were sent, read, and answered, Pemberton ordered Brig. Gen. Alexander Lawton north to Virginia with a Georgia brigade, and no attack occurred at Johns Island.

Despite the heavy weather, both sides brought in reinforcements on June 3 and 4. The 8th Michigan managed to scramble from the USS *Alabama*, which had brought the regiment from Port Royal, into the army transport, *Burnside*, despite the rough seas. The *Burnside* then delivered the Michiganders to Battery Island late on the 3rd. The Confederates brought up three units on the railroad from Savannah the following day. These were the 32nd and 47th Georgia infantry regiments and the 4th Louisiana Battalion. The reinforcements received a welcome from the Charlestonians, who nervously assumed their fate would be decided soon. The editor of the *Mercury* wrote that "were the weather less forbidding," the expected attack would likely happen any day.

Amid all this activity, more changes occurred, and confusion dominated General Pemberton's command

**This view looks west from Friars (Freers) Crossroads toward the Confederate position at the Episcopal Church. (jm)**

structure. The bad weather benefited the Confederates by preventing the Federals from being too aggressive just then.

General Gist had commanded on James Island under General Ripley. With Ripley's departure in late May, General Mercer was ordered up from Savannah and superseded both Ripley and Gist. But, while Mercer technically had been in command since May 27, he only arrived in Charleston on June 3. When Pemberton ordered Lawton's brigade north, he created a command vacancy in the Georgia district, which formerly had been under Lawton. General Mercer, who barely had time to unpack, returned to Savannah to take Lawton's place. This game of musical chairs resulted in Brig. Gen. William Duncan Smith taking command in Charleston on June 5. And it eventually brought Shanks Evans into the mix on June 15, the day before the battle of Secessionville.

One problem was that, for a few days, Gist, Mercer, and Smith all were present on James Island at the same time; then later, Gist, Smith, and Evans. Colonel Hagood sardonically noted that "things were pretty generally haphazard" and that, as all the generals (he included Evans in this) lodged in the same area at Royall's Plantation, "there was considerable unpleasantness among them, as much perhaps from the anomalous relations in command which they held toward each other, as from any other cause."

William Duncan Smith hailed from Georgia and had been a member of the star-studded West Point class of 1846. Among his classmates were Thomas J. Jackson, not then known as "Stonewall," and George B. McClellan. A. P. Hill and George Pickett also were in the class, in addition to John G. Foster and Truman Seymour, both of whom served in the Fort Sumter garrison at the beginning of the war. In total, out of 59 graduates, the class produced ten Union generals and ten Confederate generals, including all the men just named.

Upon graduating 35th of 59, Smith joined the 2nd Dragoons. He served with that unit in Mexico and through the 1850s until the Civil War. Resigning his commission in 1861, he followed his state and joined the Confederate Army. Smith arrived in Charleston on June 5 and immediately took command on James Island, where he established his headquarters a mile or so behind the Tower Battery in Secessionville.

One of the new commander's first actions was to create several forward bases on James Island along with a kind of mobile strike force which he termed his "Advanced Forces." This special brigade consisted of Col. Johnson Hagood's 1st South Carolina, Col. Clements Stevens's 24th South Carolina, Lt. Col. Charles H. Simonton's Eutaw Battalion (later the 25th South Carolina), and Lt. Col. John McEnery's 4th Louisiana Battalion. "In addition, the brigade mustered a battery of field artillery and a detail of ten or twelve cavalrymen designated for courier duty." General Smith named Col. Hagood as the commander of these Advanced Forces.

The forward bases consisted of two "Grand Guards" and their associated posts. One was located at what came to be called "Artillery Crossroads," at the intersection of today's Fort Johnson Road (formerly King's Highway) and Secessionville Road (formerly the upper portion of the Battery Island Road). The other sat about a half-mile north of that point at Friar's (or Freer's) Crossroads (where Secessionville Road intersects with Camp Road).

Small guard detachments were posted several hundred yards in advance of the Grand Guards at the Episcopalian church on Camp Road, the Presbyterian Church on Fort Johnson Road, and some three-quarters of a mile south of Artillery Crossroads on Secessionville Road near today's Bur Clare subdivision. Two of the four regiments were on duty at any given time, with the remainder camped well behind the Grand Guard sites. The forward guard detachments engaged in frequent sniping with Union patrols during the next few days.

*    *    *

On June 6, Union Brig. Gen. Wright's division rested and tried to dry out at Legareville. General Benham urged Wright to cross the men immediately to James Island. Wright had roughly two-thirds of the total force under Benham's command, and Benham felt somewhat exposed with only Stevens's division on the Confederate side of the Stono.

Not unreasonably, Benham wanted to know what he faced. He informed Stevens that he wanted a quick but thorough reconnaissance. Stevens urged caution and pointed out that the reconnaissance might be made on the eighth but would be difficult to conduct any earlier as "it will require all day tomorrow to

**This view looks south from Friars (Freers) Crossroads toward Artillery Crossroads, about one-half mile distant.** (jm)

prepare for it." Benham concurred, and Stevens began arranging a reconnaissance to go out on June 8.

In the early morning hours of June 7, Maj. Gen. Pemberton interrogated a Union prisoner whose information about the size and composition of General Benham's army prompted him to hasten the work being done on the Tower Battery. The prisoner reportedly told Pemberton that Stevens's division alone had 10,000 men, so either he deliberately exaggerated the Union numbers or Pemberton misunderstood him. Whichever it was, Pemberton ordered General Smith to "have the bombproof at Secessionville completed at once by the soldiers" and reminded Smith that "this work is important and its speedy completion necessary." And still, it rained.

The period from June 5-7 passed busily but in comparative quiet in the Federal camps. Commander Marchand wrote on June 7, "There was but little firing on the line of the Stono, probably because it has been raining nearly all day." Nonetheless, part of the 7th Connecticut under Lt. Col. Joseph Hawley went out on patrol on June 7, only hours after arriving on James Island, and briefly engaged the 24th South Carolina, then manning the Advanced Guard post at the Presbyterian Church west of Artillery Crossroads.

During this skirmish, 27-year-old Pvt. Milton Woodford of the regiment's Company A, specifically ordered by Col. Hawley to "go way out" on the company's left flank, did so and soon found himself out of sight of his comrades. As Company A was a flank company, the men carried Sharps breech-loading rifles, which could be loaded and fired faster than the standard muzzle-loading muskets. This gave the flank companies much more firepower than the other companies in a regiment. Woodford took cover behind a fence and fired several times at the Confederates. At one point, he apparently heard a bugle call but did not recognize it as "Recall." He remained in his position while the rest of his unit withdrew.

Lieutenant Colonel Capers later wrote that this unknown Union soldier "barricaded himself in a fence corner" and badly wounded one of his men. Capers decided to try to capture the soldier. Taking two men with him, he cautiously advanced within hailing distance of Woodford's position and called on him to surrender. Woodford defiantly called back that the Confederates would have to come and get him. Capers, in turn, explained that the soldier must realize he was cut off —"unsupported," as he put it—and that continued resistance likely would get him killed. Under the circumstances, Capers argued, there was no dishonor in surrendering.

No doubt pondering his tenuous position, Woodford surrendered. His Sharps rifle became an object of some curiosity among his captors, and Col. Capers kept it as a souvenir. Woodford spent some time in prison in Columbia and was exchanged later in the year.

This incident had a remarkable postscript. In 1904, then-Bishop Capers decided to try to locate his former captive and return the rifle. Woodford had died in 1887, but Capers, using the good offices of Episcopalian Bishop Chauncy Brewster of Hartford and the editors of the Hartford Courant successfully contacted Woodford's family and returned the rifle to his widow.

Another result of Col. Hawley's reconnaissance confirmed the earlier findings of Commander Marchand, who, on May 21, had visited the Grimball plantation and believed that it would be a good location both for a landing site and as a campsite for a substantial number of troops. Hawley's route had taken him inland of the plantation, and he saw what Marchand only suspected. The ground was relatively high and solid. Grimball's also gave access to the direct road across the island to Fort Johnson. Learning this and knowing that Union camps were already overcrowded on Battery Island, Brig. Gen.

Wright decided to establish a camp at Grimball's. To no one's surprise, another rainstorm hit that night, this one even more ferocious than the others, if that were possible.

Per his orders from Benham, Stevens organized a double-edged reconnaissance on June 8. The first part involved the 46th New York and a company of the 1st Massachusetts Cavalry. Colonel J. H. Morrow, an officer from Maj. Gen. Hunter's staff, was in command. The 46th was an all-German regiment, and its members, like most German immigrants, staunchly supported abolition. They had nicknamed their unit "The Fremont Regiment" after John C. Fremont, the Republican party's first presidential candidate and a firm anti-slavery advocate.

Moving up the road from Grimball's farm (part of today's Fort Johnson Road), the Fremonts and their cavalry screen advanced nearly to the church where the 7th Connecticut and Private Woodford had been the day before. There, they came under fire from the Advanced Guard pickets who belonged to the Eutaw Battalion (25th South Carolina) that day. There was a brief panic until the officers settled the men down enough to return fire. The Germans suffered two

This money was taken from the pocket of Capt. William Williams, a Georgia officer mortally wounded in the June 10 fight. (lr)

killed and five wounded, plus Col. Morrow, who fell and sprained his ankle when his horse was shot and went down. He soon decided that discretion was the better part of valor and ordered his men to break off the action and return to their camp.

Brigadier General Stevens's report of that encounter almost reads as if he is describing a diversion for what happened to the south where Capt. Hazard Stevens, the general's son and aide, led the other part of the two-pronged reconnaissance. Around 4:00 p.m., Capt. M. T. Donohoe's company of the 3rd New Hampshire, Lt. P. H. O'Rourke of the engineers, and a platoon of Massachusetts horsemen advanced across the Legare property and the causeway where the June 3 fighting had taken place. They moved past the Rivers house on the Battery Island Road where they captured four inattentive Confederate pickets from the Charleston Battalion.

The English-born Col. Edward W. Serrell commanded the 1st New York Engineers at the time of Secessionville and later served as chief engineer for all Union forces in the Department of the South. He later designed several railroad bridges in America and England. (loc)

Part of the Union patrol moved eastward "to within six or seven hundred yards" of the Tower Battery, still under construction and very much incomplete. From their position, they observed the tower itself and Fort Sumter in the distance. The other portion of the patrol advanced northward on the road. After brief, ineffectual exchanges of fire, the Federals were recalled. Neither General Stevens nor Captain Stevens reported any casualties from this foray. Unfortunately for the Yanks, the reconnaissance did not reveal to them the ground conditions immediately in front of the Tower Battery. The Confederates worked hard over the next few days to strengthen this defensive work, but the Federals' lack of terrain knowledge would cost them dearly on June 16.

There also was sporadic fighting on June 7-8 on Johns Island between Shanks Evans's men and Wright's. The 1st Massachusetts Cavalry generally participated in these actions. As it was the only mounted unit with Benham's force, its companies did service all around the area as needed.

Colonel Edward W. Serrell of the 1st New York Volunteer Engineers (and Chief Engineer in the Department of the South for much of the war) commanded a reconnaissance northward along the Johns Island side of the Stono in response to reports of Rebel activity in the area. Much of Wright's division had yet to cross to James Island because of the continual rain, and he, quite sensibly, did not want to be surprised. Serrell led portions of the 97th

Pennsylvania and the Bay State troopers northward on the 7th and skirmished to little effect with Evans's cavalry. Colonel Serrell later oversaw the construction of the "marsh battery" on Morris Island, where the famous "Swamp Angel," a 200-pounder Parrott Rifle, was mounted and from which it fired on Charleston some five miles away.

It is one of those fascinating points of contact between two historical eras that Serrell also was the maternal grandfather of General Jonathan Wainwright, the unfortunate officer who surrendered American forces in the Philippines to the Japanese in 1942.

The following evening, June 8, an instance of "friendly fire" cost the lives of four Confederates and wounded four others. Evans wrote that his cavalry pickets, falling back in front of some Federals, had shouted, "Shoot the Yankees. They are just behind." Unfortunately, the 17th South Carolina mistook some of their own horsemen for the enemy and fired on them with that tragic result.

*    *    *

Several days before the battle of Secessionville, a highly unusual form of military activity began to occur around the Union encampments on Sol Legare Island. An aerial balloon ascended for reconnaissance. Professor Thaddeus Lowe had shipped one of his "aerostats" (the official name for the balloons) to General Thomas Sherman at Port Royal the previous November. Sherman was not interested in the strange contraption, but Brig. Gen. Stevens was and had the balloon with him at the Sol Legare Island beach head.

Stevens wrote to General Benham on June 6 that he expected "to have the balloon inflated tomorrow by noon." One New Yorker wrote home, saying, "Prof. Lowe is here with his balloon, which he is now inflating, and will make a reconnaissance today." That soldier was mistaken about Lowe being there, however. On June 7, 8, and 9, "aeronaut" John B. Starkweather—not Lowe himself—made several ascensions from a location on Sol Legare Island near Battery Island in the balloon *Washington*, one of seven in Professor Lowe's aerial fleet. Starkweather made accurate observations of much of the length of the Confederate defenses on James Island.

Though an attempt had been made to conduct an aerial reconnaissance at Island Number Ten on the Mississippi River in March with the balloon *Eagle*, and even to have aeronaut John Steiner direct naval gunfire there, it had been thwarted by fog which limited the visibility too much to make the experiment useful. Union commanders in the area, skeptical of the whole idea of balloon reconnaissance since the beginning, used this failure as an excuse to get rid of Steiner and all his equipment. Sol Legare Island, therefore, became the only place outside of Virginia where aeronauts and balloons successfully performed observation during the Civil War.

# The First Heavy Blows

## CHAPTER NINE

### *JUNE 10, 1862*

General Wright's men spent June 9 crossing over to James Island, where they began spreading out and digging in all around Grimball's Plantation. They needed to dig in since the Confederates shelled them throughout the day.

The next day, June 10, was different. For one thing, the rain stopped. For another, the Confederates, until now acting largely on the defensive, came out in force and tried to dislodge the Federals from at least the northern portion of their beachhead at Grimball's. This major Confederate attack failed due to poor coordination. It nonetheless had the effect of stopping a major Union attack which had been scheduled for the following morning. Both commanders, Brig. Gen. Benham and Brig. Gen. Smith, had created complicated plans, which each proved unable to carry out.

\* \* \*

General Benham's camps stretched some three miles along the James Island shore of the Stono River from Battery Island northward to Grimball's. Stevens's division occupied the southern half of that area and Wright's the northern half. For the Confederates, Brig. Gen. Wright presented the most immediate problem as his area centered just off the road, which led directly across the island to Fort Johnson. From those Union regimental camps, Col. Hagood's Grand

**Wright's division hospital was in this area on Grimball farm, near the southern end of Wright's line.** (jm)

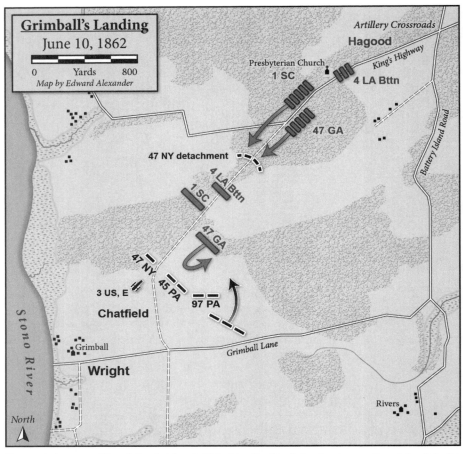

**Grimball's Landing**—Site of the fighting initiated by the Confederates in an attempt to dislodge General Wright's division from its beach head on James Island.

Guard position at Artillery Crossroads was less than 2 ½ miles distant. General Wright knew that.

Horatio Gouverneur Wright was Connecticut-born and finished second in the West Point Class of 1841. Graduating with him were several men who achieved later prominence in the war, among them John Reynolds and Richard Brooke Garnett, both killed at Gettysburg while fighting on opposite sides. In addition to them were two others who became well known in the fields of ordnance and artillery: Josiah Gorgas, later the Confederacy's Chief of Ordnance, and Thomas J. Rodman, inventor of the innovative and powerful heavy artillery pieces named for them. Wright had served as Gen. Thomas Sherman's chief engineer during the Port Royal campaign. He eventually rose to command the VI Corps in the Army of the Potomac.

On the afternoon of June 8, following Capt. Stevens's incursion toward the Tower Battery, Col. Thomas Gresham Lamar, commanding at the battery, decided to retaliate.

Lamar was from the Edgefield District in the western part of South Carolina across the Savannah River from Augusta, Georgia. He had become prominent as a planter and member of the state legislature before the war. He served briefly on the staff of Governor Pickens but pressed for field service and soon found himself on Morris Island in command of a battery. By the spring of 1862, he had organized another battery in Edgefield, brought it to Charleston, and seen it grow into the Second South Carolina Artillery.

Lamar's cannoneers manned several of the defensive positions in addition to the Tower Battery. The colonel had them open on the Union positions all along the line. This continued for several hours and through much of June 9. Commander Marchand, on the *James Adger*, heard them. "The Rebel batteries on James Island," he wrote, "have been firing all day at intervals towards our troops or gunboats in the Stono." He did not know it, but the "Rebel batteries" mainly targeted General Wright's camps.

However, Maj. Gen. Pemberton disapproved of this extensive barrage and thought it unnecessary. "Don't allow your command, especially the batteries, to waste ammunition," he wrote to General Gist for referral to Col. Lamar. "They must not fire merely

Historic structures have disappeared, but the Grimball house was located in this area. To the right were slave quarters. (jm)

A road parallels the Stono River on the right through the trees. General Wright's camps stretched for some three miles along the river. (cm)

**Located on the Stono River, Wright's camps and earthworks formed the left of the Union positions on James Island. Wright's headquarters was in this area. (jm)**

because they are fired at. The large guns must not waste their ammunition." Colonel Lamar, apparently with some reluctance, cut back on his rate of fire. Pemberton's concern was warranted, as ammunition of all kinds had been in relatively short supply for several months.

By this time, Brig. Gen. Benham had decided that destroying the Secessionville battery would be the only way to stop this kind of bombardment. Clearly, the tower was doing for the Rebs what the balloon had done for the Yanks—spotting for the artillery and providing all the information the gunners needed to accurately shell their targets. Destroying it seemed the only option. Wright, believing the Federals to be drastically outnumbered, opposed the idea.

Commander Drayton, as pessimistic as ever about the army, wrote to Commodore Du Pont on June 10 that "it does not seem to me that the spirit that leads to victory is prevalent, nor do I think that Benham commands the confidence of his subordinates." In that last reflection, at least, he certainly was correct. Captain Lusk of General Stevens's staff expressed a common view when he wrote to his mother, "Right or wrong, all despise (Benham). No one trusts him. If we take Charleston, it will not be his fault."

Drayton also feared that the near constant fire support he had been providing at Wright's request was taking its toll on his guns. "The Parrott guns of the squadron are completely used up," he told Du Pont, explaining that many of the vent pieces had either "blown out entirely" or expanded in size and could not last much longer.

Still, Benham wanted to attack and convinced General Hunter to agree. Attack they would, according to a three-pronged plan which it seems in retrospect was almost guaranteed to fail.

General Benham began by asking Commander Drayton if he might provide five gunboats to provide fire support at various points along the river.

With the gunboats in place, General Stevens would move "two good regiments, supported by two pieces of artillery" across the marsh and causeway where the fighting had occurred on June 3. This column, some time "between 3 o'clock and the earliest daylight" (on June 11), would rush and capture a Confederate battery believed to be in the area, then begin moving north on the Battery Island Road. This would put that force on today's Secessionville Road, near the Rivers house and roughly a thousand yards in front of the Tower Battery.

At the same time, "a selected regiment" from Wright's division would move forward along the (Fort Johnson) road toward the Presbyterian Church and prepare to attack once, but not before, it heard the fighting between Stevens's men and the Rebels. That force would then launch its attack and prevent the Confederates there from turning south and hitting Stevens.

While this proceeded, Col. Robert Williams of the 1st Massachusetts Cavalry would take "two good regiments and two pieces of artillery" on a leftward sweep around the Presbyterian Church, link up with Wright's "selected regiment," take command of the whole, then decide whether to proceed or withdraw. The order states that Williams should start "soon after 3 o'clock p.m." though that obviously meant 3:00 a.m.

*This view from Grimball farm looks south along the line of Wright's camps. The Stono River is approximately 100 yards through the trees on the right. (jm)*

*Confederates maintained an advance guard near the modern site of the James Island Presbyterian Church. (jm)*

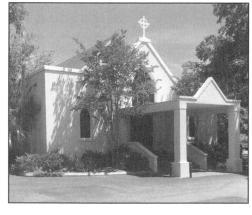

Col. John Chatfield commanded the 6th Connecticut and the First Brigade of General Wright's division. He was responsible for the deployment of Union troops who successfully repulsed the Confederate attack of June 10. (loc)

Somehow, the columns of Stevens and Wright would link up and move to intercept any Confederates that Colonel Williams's men drove from their positions. All these plans should be completed before dawn, in heavily wooded country, and coordinated with the use of "distinctive colored rockets" to be provided by the navy; colored rockets which Benham even stated in his order the navy did not have. In the end, Benham's overly complicated plan did not fail, but this was only because it never happened. The Confederates pre-empted it with an attack of their own on June 10.

The purpose of the Confederate attack was to "drive the enemy and seize and hold the line of the clearing," in order to break up Wright's camps along the river and deploy artillery to "drive the gunboats from the landing."

Fortunately for the Federals on the morning of June 10, Col. John Chatfield of the 6th Connecticut, commanding his own regiment and the 47th New York, had positioned his pickets well. Wright's main picket line was posted about half a mile out on the road leading to the Presbyterian Church. Colonel Chatfield then placed a small detachment, perhaps 15 men, from the 47th New York another quarter mile or so in advance of that. They acted as the tripwire.

Confederate scouts began probing the line early in the morning, but Union pickets saw them and drove them back. Sporadic firing from the pickets continued until around 2:00 p.m., when Confederate artillery opened a concentrated barrage lasting 90 minutes. During that time, the 47th Georgia, 1st South Carolina, and 4th Louisiana Battalion lined up and prepared to advance. The Georgians moved on the left of the road, the Carolinians on the right, and the Louisiana boys followed up in reserve.

Around 3:30, the Rebs moved forward, driving the advanced Federal pickets before them and apparently mistaking the withdrawal of these men for a more general retreat. The two leading Confederate regiments—rightly not wanting to advance on the road where they could easily be seen—came through the thick woods to the sides. This slowed them down and broke up their line so that the 47th Georgia soon found itself considerably ahead of the 1st South Carolina without realizing it. This advance must have taken quite some time as Col. Chatfield said it started "early on the evening of the 10th," and Commander Marchand described it as "a night attack." Whatever

the hour, the 47th Georgia was about to see the elephant for the first time, and it would not be a pleasant experience.

Finally getting through the woods at about 4:30, the Georgians entered a clearing at the other end of the Union line to which the pickets had retreated. Colonel Henry Ruhl Guss of the 97th Pennsylvania commanded a battle line consisting of two companies of his regiment, two of the 45th Pennsylvania, and one of the 47th New York. On seeing the Confederates, the Union troops fired a volley which cut down several men, including Capt. William W. Williams of Company C. The Rebs tried to push forward but finally fell back into the cover of the woods where they regrouped.

The Federals soon were reinforced by other companies of the 97th Pennsylvania, who swung around onto the left flank of the Georgians, and by four guns of Company E, Third U.S. Artillery. Not long after this, the navy began firing over the soldiers' heads into the woods where the Confederates had taken cover.

The Georgia boys were not finished, however, as their regimental commander, Col. Gilbert Williams, older brother of the fallen Capt. Williams, sent them forward a second time. However, the result was the same. The concentrated musketry, augmented by Dunbar's regular artillery, part of the 3rd Rhode Island Heavy Artillery, and the navy's guns overwhelmed the attack. A few men got within ten yards of the Federal line, but the regiment was forced to withdraw again, leaving more of its dead and wounded in the clearing.

The Confederates suffered 60-70 casualties, with the Federals burying 16 of them and bringing several wounded to the hospital for care. Three men of the

**In this view, the main house of the Grimball farm is approximately one-quarter mile ahead. General Wright's camps are ahead and to both sides of the road.** (jm)

**This view of the church site looks toward Union lines.** (jm)

97th Pennsylvania were killed and about a dozen other Union troops wounded.

* * *

The failure of the June 10 attack resulted in harsh words between Maj. Gen. Pemberton and Brig. Gen. Smith. Pemberton considered having Smith, who had been in command on James Island for only three days, arrested. Cooler heads prevailed, but this blowup between the Confederate commanders preceded another larger blowup between Union Brig. Gen. Benham and his subordinates a week later. Tensions ran high on both sides of the lines.

The June 10 attack had a more immediate effect on the conduct of overall Union operations. Though a clear tactical victory for the Federals, it proved to be a strategic win for the Confederates as it seems to have convinced Maj. Gen. Hunter that the Rebel forces were much stronger, and his own much weaker, than he had believed. If they weren't much stronger, he thought, they would not have attacked at all. While Benham was unconcerned about this, what happened on June 10 gave Hunter pause. His men already had been on James Island for a week without making the quick, determined advance that Benham's plan had called for and which everyone on both sides had expected. Hunter blamed this on a lack of boat transportation, though the weather had played a significant role. In any case, he slammed on the brakes immediately after the Grimball skirmishing. He became concerned both about his numbers and about the condition of his men. General Wright and the navy agreed.

Wright wrote to Commander Drayton on June 11, then again on June 12, asking, indeed pleading, that "the whole naval force should be retained here until our position on this island should be more assured" and suggesting that "it would be unwise to diminish our present force, either naval or military by a single man or gun, until reinforcements arrive."

Commander Marchand wrote in his journal on June 13 about "the helpless condition of the army" on James Island. "The gunboats then," he said, "are in reality the only obstacle to prevent their being driven out."

Marchand may have been exaggerating slightly, but perhaps because he feared this very thing, Hunter decided to return to the main headquarters at Hilton Head. He later explained this in a report to

Secretary of War Edwin Stanton with nothing more than a boilerplate statement that "matters affecting the safety of the command in other portions of the department" required him to leave. This was hardly an adequate explanation, and other factors almost surely contributed. Some historians have suggested, though perhaps only half in jest, that Hunter wanted to see his wife, who had been at Hilton Head for some time.

At this point, Hunter's fate was being discussed because of his earlier emancipation edict, which President Lincoln had rescinded. Talk swirled around Washington that he would be relieved of his command, and Benham named to replace him. On June 9, Representative Charles A. Wickliffe of Kentucky had introduced a resolution directing Stanton to investigate whether Hunter had armed slaves.

Hunter must have heard the rumors of his dismissal and may have learned of Wickliffe's action. It seems reasonable that concern over these possibilities factored into his decision to return to Hilton Head.

Perhaps more concerning than the rumors was the fact that Stanton had telegraphed Hunter on June 9 with what could at best be called unenthusiastic support. Informing him that there could be no reinforcements until after Richmond fell, whenever that might be, Stanton wrote, "you are authorized at your discretion to operate with the Navy in the operations against Charleston, so far as the forces now under your command will permit." In other words, Hunter was on his own.

The writer has come to believe that Hunter, like General Hooker at Chancellorsville, simply had lost, if not his nerve, then at least his confidence in himself and the James Island operation. Be that as it may, he wrote to General Benham on June 10, the evening of the Grimball skirmishing, saying, "You will make no attempt to advance on Charleston or to attack Fort Johnson until largely re-enforced or until you receive specific instructions from these headquarters to that effect."

This is a strangely worded order. "Until largely re-enforced" is curiously passive phrasing because no such reinforcements would have come without Hunter's orders, and Benham obviously would have known that. Had such orders come, their purpose could only have been an attack on Fort Johnson.

After instructing Benham to "provide for a secure intrenched encampment" and to make "all proper arrangements" for its security and supply, Maj. Gen. Hunter went on to say something extraordinary, the implications of which have been largely unremarked by historians. "If you can safely leave," he wrote, "you will return to your usual headquarters at Hilton Head." He said nothing about Benham returning to James Island.

Why would Hunter do this? Benham did not need to leave his command for at least the two full days it would have taken for him to report in person and return to James Island, especially if the Confederates were being reinforced, as Hunter suspected. Benham would have been sending regular updates to Hunter anyway. By ordering Benham to prepare to leave, Hunter seemed to have given up on the entire James Island operation nearly a week before the battle of Secessionville.

The image of Hunter penning this order from his headquarters aboard the army transport ship, *Delaware*, shortly before his departure conjures up a similar image of Maj. Gen. George McClellan sitting on a transport in the James River, justifying his "change of base," which happened in conjunction with the strategically disastrous Seven Days battles. It seems clear that General Hunter had been badly shaken.

Flag Officer Du Pont certainly thought along these lines on Sunday, June 15, when General and Mrs. Hunter attended church services and then dinner aboard the USS *Wabash*. During dinner, the general received a message ordering him to transfer his cavalry and an infantry regiment north. Hunter, wrote Du Pont to his wife, "was much put out and said he would withdraw all the troops from James Island." The order was almost immediately rescinded, but Hunter's reaction shows how ready he was to give up the entire project.

\*　　\*　　\*

The aftermath of the June 10 fighting also produced one of those moments of tender humanity that often arises in war, perhaps, especially during the American Civil War, which stand out enough to be acknowledged by the enemy. One thinks immediately of Sgt. Richard Kirkland, the "Angel of Marye's Heights," at Fredericksburg.

In this instance, however, it involved Maj. Henry Sessions of the 3rd Rhode Island Heavy Artillery and Capt. William Williams of the 47th Georgia. Captain Williams, as noted, fell seriously wounded during his regiment's first push.

But the story is best told as it was written by Major Sessions and acknowledged by the editors of the Charleston *Daily Courier* on July 9:

> *A Rare Case*—It is our pleasure and privilege to record the fact that there was one officer among the Yankees on James' Island not devoid of the principles of honorable warfare.
>
> A communication to the Editor of the Savannah News gives a copy of a letter written by a Yankee officer to the wife of Capt. Williams, of Georgia, who fell in the desperate skirmish of the 10th of June.
>
> The letter is as follows:
>
> Headquarters Second Battalion,
> Third Regiment R.I. Artillery,
> James' Island, June 19th, 1862.
> Mrs. Roxanna Williams:
>
> Madam—It is with sorrow I communicate to you the death of your husband, Captain W. W. Williams, who died on the 11th instant from the effect of severe wounds received in an engagement with our forces on the 10th inst., (Tuesday).
>
> Capt. Williams' wounds were of such a nature that surgical aid could not save him; they were in his breast, and our own surgeon could do no more for him than to relieve his sufferings by administering annodines (sic).
>
> I can assure you that your husband had every care and attention we could bestow. He was rational to the last, and expressed the greatest solicitude for yourself. He exacted from the writer a promise to communicate to you his situation, and make known to you that his last thoughts were of you.
>
> Capt. Williams signified a desire to see a minister of the gospel. One of our Chaplains visited him, and was in communion and prayer with him for an hour or two preceding his death, and is satisfied that your husband

was prepared to enter a better world, where the wounded and suffering rejoice in heavenly bliss.

Capt. Williams did not suffer much. He began to fail at about nine o'clock, P.M., his strength gradually failing him, and at one o'clock, A.M., 11th inst., he breathed his last.

Trusting that God may give you strength to bear your misfortune with fortitude and courage,

I am, very respectfully,

Henry Sessions,

Major Third Regiment R.I. Artillery.

This letter was passed to the Confederates via a flag of truce on June 20 and, presumably, then forwarded to Mrs. Williams. Moreover, as the captain was found to be a Mason, several of his Masonic brothers on the Union side arranged a truce and returned his body to their compatriots on the Confederate side, likely with appropriate Masonic rituals. The fact that the Georgia officer and his wife had eight children makes the entire story especially poignant.

\*    \*    \*

The day after the fight at Grimball's, General Pemberton was worried. Receiving yet another request from Richmond for reinforcements, he responded to George Randolph, the Confederate Secretary of War, brusquely telling him to stop asking for more troops from Charleston. "I not only cannot spare any more troops from this department," Pemberton said, "but there is danger here unless I am re-enforced."

In a nervous and exasperated tone, he then warned General Smith that the Federals remained in place from the previous day and had been reinforced to two full regiments and ten pieces of artillery. Wanting Smith to keep pressing the Yankees, he urged "constant skirmishing" and asked if Smith either could take the enemy's batteries or at least do something to "derange his plans." The first scheme would have required more men than had been used in the unsuccessful attack on the previous day.

Pemberton then suggested something quite unusual—a kind of chemical warfare—when he asked Smith to look into setting fire to the woods west of

Secessionville. "You can get resin and turpentine and the wind is favorable." In short, anything would be permissible to drive the Union troops away from their threatening position astride the road that led to Fort Johnson. As a footnote, he instructed Brig. Gen. Smith to order Col. Lamar to stop wasting ammunition by firing on the gunboats.

Finally, he instructed Shanks Evans on Johns Island to send at least one regiment, "more if you can," to help defend James Island.

Pemberton was not the only one worrying. William Porcher Miles, Charleston's delegate to the Confederate House of Representatives (and, incidentally, the designer of the well-known banner which became the Army of Northern Virginia battle flag), wanted General Pemberton replaced and wrote this to General Lee. In a lengthy telegram, also on June 11, he told Lee that "Pemberton does not possess the confidence of his officers, his troops, or the people of Charleston." Miles warned that a petition started by "some of our best and most influential citizens" sought another commander. Miles suggested General Smith as Pemberton's replacement. Two weeks later, Lee referred the matter to President Davis, saying, "I hardly see how the removal of Pemberton can be avoided."

Lee was right. It could not be avoided, though Pemberton's transfer would not happen until October when, having been promoted to lieutenant general, he took command of the defenses of Vicksburg. General P. G. T. Beauregard, who had been Charleston's first Confederate military commander, stepped in as the replacement, partially because of his popularity in the city. For now, however, Pemberton remained in command.

From this point, as Patrick Brennan poetically noted, Major General David Hunter "floats through the James Island Campaign like a detached phantom, nominally in charge of the Union effort but exerting little, if any, influence." Hunter left on June 12 for Hilton Head. General Benham, though under orders not "to advance on Charleston or to attack Fort Johnson," now took charge and no doubt pondered how best to "provide for a secure intrenched encampment."

At least it had stopped raining.

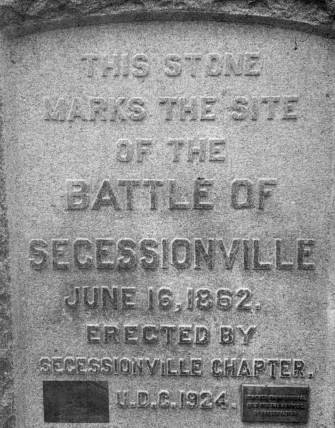

THIS STONE
MARKS THE SITE
OF THE
BATTLE OF
SECESSIONVILLE
JUNE 16, 1862.
ERECTED BY
SECESSIONVILLE CHAPTER.
U.D.C. 1924.

# The Council of War

## CHAPTER TEN

*JUNE 10–15, 1862*

Both sides spent the next few days after the June 10 fighting constructing batteries, mounting guns, and sporadically exchanging fire. Brigadier General Wright's Federals strengthened their defensive lines in front of Grimball's. Stevens's men pushed forward on Sol Legare Island past the site of the June 3 skirmish and mounted guns in earthwork positions to cover the area between the causeway and the Tower Battery.

For example, the men of the 79th New York spent June 13 and 14 constructing two earthwork batteries, allowing them to "jaw back" at the Confederate guns that had been bothering them. The Union battery "on the extreme right of our line protected by one of the many impassable swamps with which the surrounding country was filled" came to be called Battery Stevens. This battery and Battery Williams, several hundred yards to the left, were armed with 30-pounder Parrott rifles, though Battery Stevens also had one of the unusual 64-pounder "James Rifles."

These odd pieces were obsolete 32-pounder smoothbores of a type usually mounted in seacoast fortifications or on large warships because of their weight (7,500 pounds). They very rarely appeared in the field. A few were rifled as experiments, a process which doubled the throw-weight of their projectiles, thus making them into 64-pounders. James Rifles were manufactured in various sizes, but these early war expedients only were used until specifically designed rifled artillery pieces became available in

This photo of the battle marker in the kiosk area of the Fort Lamar Heritage Preserve faces toward the Confederate right. (jm)

large numbers. The one in Battery Stevens had been used in the earlier bombardment of Fort Pulaski.

Meanwhile, the Confederates kept busy on the Tower Battery, adding height to the walls and depth to the ditch in front. They also built entrenchments and a substantial abatis near the Advanced Forces position south of Artillery Crossroads. These latter works allowed them a clear field of fire should the Yanks move up the Battery Island Road again as they had done on June 8.

The two sides continued to fire at each other, causing remarkably few casualties. One Reb was killed when a shell passed through five Confederate tents in the Charleston Battalion's camp behind the Tower Battery, taking his life as he relaxed while reading in his tent. Another odd fatality occurred when one of the Highlanders was "seen to fall as a shot passed." Though his body was completely unmarked, he died, "and it was popularly supposed that the wind of the ball had taken the breath from his body." This rare occurrence may have been the result of a "spontaneous pneumothorax," or lung collapse, which sometimes is associated with drastic changes in air pressure, which can be caused by artillery fire.

Opposing pickets also sustained occasional injuries from the musketry. Private James Chase, Company F, 3rd New Hampshire, fell wounded in the leg by a Confederate picket on the evening of

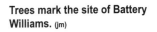

**Trees mark the site of Battery Williams.** (jm)

June 15 while his company reconnoitered ahead of the Union lines and helped to cover the ground in front of Batteries Williams and Stevens. Later that evening, the New Hampshire regiment's pickets got so far forward that "some of our men actually found themselves posted on the wrong side of the rebels." Apparently, they fell back quickly enough to avoid alerting Colonel Lamar's pickets.

In any case, the firing by both sides during those days became nearly as regular as the rain had been earlier; "a fight at long taw," as one writer put it. One Union soldier wrote that the Confederate battery had "irritated our camps with shell" and the Federals certainly did their best to irritate the Rebel camps as well. With June 16 fast approaching, it was all about to come to a head.

*     *     *

On June 15, yet another change occurred in the Confederate command structure. Major General Pemberton issued an order that day, stating that Brig. Gen. Evans "is hereby assigned to duty in the First Division, First Military District of Department South Carolina and Georgia. He will exercise the command thereof until further orders." That last sentence indicated this would be a temporary command. Several days prior to this, Pemberton had ordered Evans to send "as many infantry troops as you can spare *for temporary service*" (author's emphasis). This offers a hint about his intentions. It was Pemberton's way of getting around a touchy issue of seniority.

Pemberton wanted the troops that Evans would bring with him, but as Evans was senior to Brig. Gen. Smith, Smith could not have retained command of the district with Evans present. However, Evans still commanded the Second District, which encompassed Johns Island. Thus Pemberton, depending on how one reads the order, apparently put him in command of the first "division" of the First District, though everyone seems to have assumed that he held overall command of the district.

What Colonel Hagood—who could not abide Evans and thought him nothing more than a common drunk—called the "anomalous relations in command" obviously created as many problems as they solved, but they all apparently were worth it to General Pemberton.

This was not the first time that Shanks Evans had been in an "anomalous" command situation. Just a year before, on June 18, 1861, then-Major Nathan Evans had been ordered to "conduct (the Fourth South Carolina under Col. J. B. E. Sloan) to Leesburg, Va., to report to Col. Eppa Hunton." For reasons still unclear, Colonel Hunton and others understood Major Evans to be in command of all Confederate forces in Loudoun County, Virginia. Evans was consistently referred to as "General" Evans during that month before First Manassas. General Beauregard even spoke of the "patriotic conduct" of Colonels Hunton and Sloan in their relations with Major Evans and expressed the hope to Evans that their good relationship would "put out of sight the anomalous position you are placed in."

In the final event, those problems were resolved, and things worked themselves out with Brig. Gen. Benham's attack on the Tower Battery. That happened the day after Evans took command, and neither he nor Brig. Gen. Smith were directly involved in the fighting in any significant way. Evans disappeared soon thereafter and was back in effective command on Johns Island by June 21. Indeed, the departmental organizational table for June 1862 lists General Smith in command of the First District (though, curiously, his name is followed by a question mark) and General Evans in command of the Second District. There is no mention of Evans in connection with the First District. Perhaps to lay any confusion to rest, General Pemberton formally assigned, or rather reassigned, General Smith to the command of the First Military District on July 8.

Not long after that, Evans transferred north. On July 17, Shanks took command of the 17th, 18th, and 23rd South Carolina infantry regiments, plus Capt. Robert Boyce's South Carolina battery and Capt. Walter Leake's Virginia battery and reported with that newly formed brigade to the Army of Northern Virginia.

For a brief time, though, the situation was rather confused. As historian Patrick Brennan wrote, "Both command structures sagged under their own self-inflicted weaknesses—the Confederates being top heavy with too many generals, and the Federals floundering without one."

\*    \*    \*

What happened on June 16 appears to have been a somewhat truncated and perhaps slightly more realistic version of General Benham's plan for the abortive June 11 attack.

On the June 15, as the Confederates kept digging in, Brig. Gen. Benham's men drew rations and ammunition. They quickly figured out why. Soldiers being soldiers, they knew that the officers had something planned, and it had to involve that pesky Confederate battery with the tall tower to the rear. June 15 fell on a Sunday, so the chaplains stayed abnormally busy with formal and informal prayer and worship services, tinged with a special urgency.

That evening Benham summoned Generals Stevens and Wright and Colonel (Acting Brigadier General) Williams to meet with him aboard the *Delaware*. Commander Drayton also was present, and it is largely from his recollections of the meeting that historians have been able to get a reasonably clear idea of what occurred. In the aftermath of the defeat, the army officers tended to focus on assigning blame to each other. Precisely who said what at the meeting devolved into significant controversy, with Benham saying that Stevens and Wright had supported his decision to attack, while Stevens and Wright claimed they had not.

They gathered aboard the ship, and Brig. Gen. Benham told them around 9:00 p.m. of his decision to attack. This was not unexpected. However, the timing took them all by surprise. Benham ordered that the attack take place before dawn the next day. This gave them only a few hours to return to their camps, brief their subordinate commanders, make final preparations, organize the order of march, and still leave the men a little time to get some sleep.

At this meeting, Brig. Gen. Stevens later insisted that he, Wright, and Williams were "unmistakably opposed" to Brig. Gen. Benham's plan. Stevens also said that he had strongly urged Benham to delay the attack until later in the day, preferably the afternoon, and to precede it with an artillery barrage from his own batteries and the gunboats. In response to this, Benham agreed only that the Union troops should move out around 4:00 a.m. instead of 3:00 a.m. as he initially had wanted. According to Benham, Stevens's request for a delay was the only objection to his plan expressed by any of the other officers.

Yet, according to Stevens, when Benham asked Wright for his opinion of the operation, Wright "answered that he would make his reply in the shape of certain interrogatories to me."

Wright first asked whether Stevens's artillery "had impaired the strength of the enemy's works at Secessionville." Stevens replied that it had not. Wright then asked whether Stevens knew "of any instance where volunteer troops have successfully stormed works as strong" as those at Secessionville. Stevens did not. Finally, following up on the previous question, which reflected his lack of confidence in his own troops, Wright asked if Stevens believed that "the present case" would be any different; in other words, did he believe that the Federals could take the Tower Battery. Stevens replied that he considered only "a bare possibility" of success. Wright then turned to Benham and said, "There, General, you have my opinion."

Indeed, Wright wrote to Hunter on June 22 that he "emphatically" repudiated "any attempt to use my name as favoring the operations of the 16th instant." Stevens wrote to Hunter on the same day, saying the same thing.

Stevens also insisted that he and Wright had urged Benham to recognize that he was ordering them to fight a battle. While true, it should be remembered that Maj. Gen. Hunter did not instruct Benham not to fight a battle, but only not to advance on Charleston or Fort Johnson, which Benham did not do.

Moreover, he had been ordered to secure his camps. Given that the Tower Battery had been shelling those camps for several days, an attack designed to silence it hardly seems to have been a violation of Hunter's orders. Hunter wrote to Secretary of War Stanton that he had ordered "no advance should be made" but, as the reader has seen, his orders to Benham were rather more specific than that.

Benham nonetheless danced around this distinction after the fact, writing that he had felt "fully authorized in taking (the Tower Battery), if possible, by a direct attack." That clearly implies a battle, but a few lines later, in the same paragraph, he referred to the operation as "a reconnaissance upon the fort." Hunter, Benham, Stevens, and Wright all played the blame game after the incident.

That is why Commander Drayton's recollections are so important. Benham wrote to him on June 17, asking about this. Drayton replied the following day, at the same time sending a full report to Commodore Du Pont. His frustration appeared clearly in this report when he wrote, "There seems to be a good deal of recrimination going on here, everyone laying the blame of defeat on everyone else."

In his response to Benham, Drayton showed that he did not want to get caught in the middle of the army's internal squabble. He diplomatically explained that he could remember "no direct objections" except Stevens's comment about the timing.

Still, Drayton reminded Benham of General Wright's "interrogatories" to Stevens and concluded that he "must confess that the impression was made on me by the general tone of the conversation that while expressing every desire to further your views to the utmost of their power, the three officers above named [Stevens, Wright, and Williams] were scarcely in favor of the movement."

All of this, of course, would be played out in army channels in the weeks and months following the battle. Before that happened, however, the assault on what would become known as Fort Lamar was about to take place.

# One of the Decisive Engagements of the War

## CHAPTER ELEVEN

### JUNE 16, 1862

The Secessionville peninsula is formed by Secessionville Creek to the south and what now is called Seaside Creek to the north. This can be confusing as wartime sources sometimes referred to modern Seaside Creek as Simpson's Creek and sometimes as Lighthouse Creek. There is a modern Simpson's Creek about two miles to the north and a modern Lighthouse Creek about that distance to the east and south.

Both Secessionville Creek and Seaside Creek are narrow, twisting waterways bordered by extensive pluff mud marshes. The peninsula itself, from where it effectively begins at the old Battery Island Road (that section today is called Old Military Road) to where it turns into marsh and merges with the waters of Clark Sound, is approximately one and a half miles in length and is shaped like an hourglass. At its widest point, not far from where it begins, it is less than a half-mile.

The Confederates constructed the Tower Battery at the narrowest part of the peninsula, where there was solid ground for perhaps 130 yards between the creek marshes. The battery was a roughly M-shaped earthwork of a type known in the terminology of field fortifications as a "priest cap." This is defined as "a detached earthwork consisting of two faces joined in a reentrant (the "V" shape at the center of the "M") and two long flanks (the sides or legs of the "M") extending toward the rear and inclining away from the open gorge (the rear)." Thus, the rear of the earthwork

**From here inside the Tower Battery on the Confederate right, the 4th Louisiana position looked out across the marsh. The Louisianans engaged the 3rd New Hampshire.** (cm)

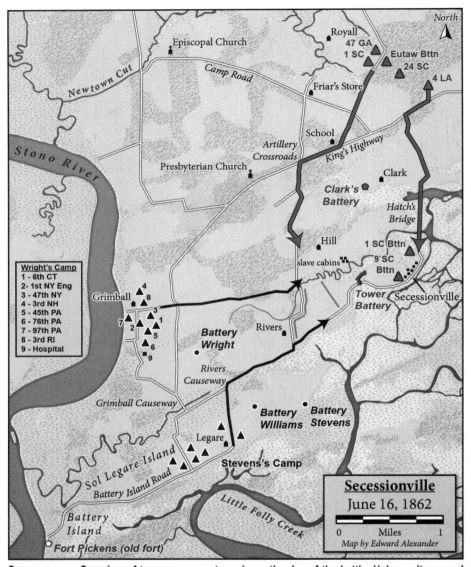

SECESSIONVILLE—**Overview of troop movements early on the day of the battle. Union units moved eastward from their camps on the Stono River toward Secessionville. Confederate units man the Tower Battery and advance southward on the Union flank.**

would be wider than the front facing the enemy. The Tower Battery faced a little south of westward, as if the M were lying on its left side.

Such a design allows the defenders to converge their fire onto attackers at angles which gives them not only a wider field of fire overall but allows each

Near here, the 8th Michigan advanced before dawn on June 16 and engaged Confederate pickets. (jm)

angle of the reentrant to overlap with the other. With the Tower Battery located at the narrow waist of the Secessionville peninsula, the fortification pinched the Union attackers into an even smaller area than that dictated by the width of the peninsula itself, making them a better target for the defenders.

Eventually, the Confederates mounted 13 guns in the battery, but on June 16, only five or six guns and a mortar were in place; accounts vary. The guns were an 8-inch "Columbiad" smoothbore, two rifled 24-pounders, and two or three smoothbore 18-pounders. One or two of the 18-pounders did not see action during the fight.

The Rebels may have used the 10-inch mortar. Colonel Lamar noted in his after-action report that Lt. William S. Barton "displayed great skill and coolness in the management of the mortar, which had considerable effect upon the enemy." A newspaper account by "EYE-WITNESS" (who may have been Lamar himself) says that Lt. Barton served the mortar "with admirable skill." There are no further

General Stevens's attacking force staged here for its assault on the Tower Battery. (jm)

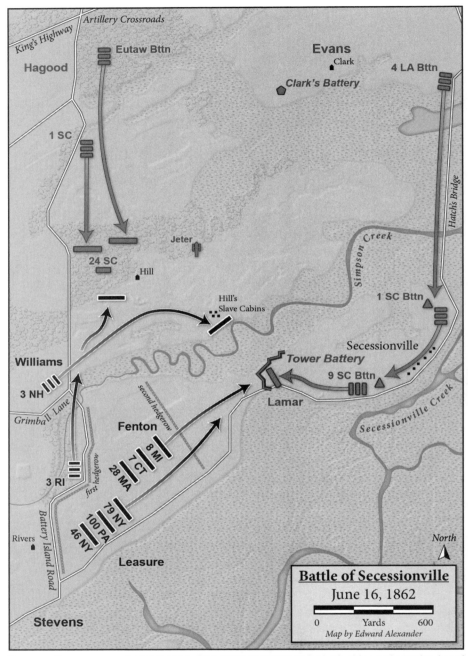

**Battle of Secessionville—**A closer view of the troop movements by both sides early on the day of the fighting.

This view looks toward Union lines where a modern road cuts through the Confederate right. (jm)

details, however, and the writer has found no Union source that mentions the attackers coming under mortar fire. Given the very short range and the fact that the Federals would have been able to see the mortar rounds in the air, it is curious that none of the Yanks commented on it, especially if this fire had "considerable effect" on them.

\*    \*    \*

At 2:00 a.m. on June 16, as the Union troops began to stir, the Confederates under Col. Thomas Lamar were hard at work strengthening the walls of the Tower Battery. In fact, the men had been laboring steadily at this since Maj. Gen. Pemberton had impressed on Brig. Gen. W.D. Smith the necessity of completing the bombproof immediately behind the forward wall of the battery more than a week before.

On the night of the 15th and in the early hours of the 16th, working part of the time in the rain, Lamar's men did their usual labor and, following orders from Brig. Gen. Evans, mounted additional guns moved from Capt. Bonneau's "gunboat" or floating battery. This order seemed to have been given because the "hulk battery," as Brig. Gen. Benham called it, had been set on fire and damaged by shells fired from Battery Stevens.

Captain Bonneau later commanded the blockade runner, *Ella and Annie*, until her capture and his imprisonment in November 1863. The vessel, a 1,400-ton sidewheel steamer, was renamed the USS *Malvern* and became Admiral David Dixon Porter's flagship for the remainder of the war.

The soldiers working so diligently on the Tower Battery came mostly from Companies B and I of Lamar's 1st South Carolina Artillery. Lamar's unit was redesignated as the 2nd South Carolina Artillery

**Col. Thomas G. Lamar commanded the Tower Battery during much of the battle. Dying from malaria later in 1862, General Pemberton honored him by having the battery renamed "Fort Lamar."** (pb)

in August 1862 and kept that name for the rest of the war.

Commanded respectively by Capts. Samuel J. Reed and George D. Keitt (older brother of former US Congressman Lawrence M. Keitt, who had been involved in the famous Sumner-Brooks caning incident on the Senate floor in 1856), those two companies had dug a seven-foot deep ditch by the morning of the battle. Their efforts also raised nine-foot-high walls, and an abatis of fallen trees fronted the whole fortification. The soldiers shortly expected a relief work party from Col. Spartan Goodlett's 22nd South Carolina.

This detachment of 100 men under Capt. Joshua Jamison marched out to help mount Captain Bonneau's guns. By 3:00, however, it still had not arrived (marching in the rain had slowed the men down), so Col. Lamar, having pushed his men as hard as he could, finally allowed them to lay down and get some sleep. Their weapons were stacked well behind them. Colonel Lamar later somewhat sheepishly admitted that this was the first time since he had been in command of the battery that he had allowed his men to sleep without their weapons by their sides. Lamar himself, after "superintending all night the operations of (the) working party, and exhausted had fallen asleep upon the parapet" about 3:30. Neither he nor his men slept for very long.

\*    \*    \*

By 3:30, Brig. Gen. Stevens's division, numbering 3,562 men, formed and prepared to move forward. This force included the cannoneers and four guns—two 12-pounder field howitzers and two James Rifles—from Capt. Alfred Rockwell's 1st Connecticut Light Artillery.

Absolute silence was the order of the day for all concerned. The cannoneers even muffled the wheels of their guns to avoid making any noise that might alert the Confederate pickets as the Federals approached. The task for the foot soldiers: assault the Tower Battery itself. For this, they were "not to fire a shot, but rely exclusively on the bayonet, the muskets to be loaded but not capped." Many men ignored that order.

Stevens's aide, Lt. Benjamin R. Lyons—along with "a negro guide" whose name has been lost to history and the storming party or "forlorn hope" consisting of Companies C, Capt. Ralph Ely, and Company H, Capt. Richard Doyle, of the 8th Michigan—led this risky and daring endeavor. A detachment from Company E of the New York engineers under Capt. Alfred F. Sears also moved ahead.

In addition to clearing any obstacles that might hinder the supporting troops, the engineers cut embrasures in the thick hedge lining the first of two drainage ditches crossing the field. This created an artillery position for Captain Rockwell's guns. The two advanced Michigan companies acted as the shock troops whose momentum hopefully would carry them over the walls and open the way for the rest of General Stevens's division.

Colonel William M. Fenton commanded the 8th Michigan, the only western regiment in David Hunter's army. He was a former lieutenant governor of the state (and failed candidate for governor) and namesake of the town of Fenton, Michigan, which he had helped establish in the 1830s. His regiment had seen action previously, engaged in a sharp fight against the 13th Georgia near Fort Pulaski on April 16, two months to the day before Secessionville. They had an idea about what lay ahead. In that earlier fight, ten of Fenton's men had been killed.

The colonel also commanded Stevens's first brigade, consisting of his own Michiganders, the 7th Connecticut, and the 28th Massachusetts. Because of this, Lt. Col. Frank Graves led the 8th into battle. Initially, the Massachusetts men had been placed second in the assaulting column, but Fenton had them switch places with the 7th Connecticut because their reliability remained doubtful based on their performance in the June 3 skirmish on Sol Legare Island.

**This is the site of the breakthrough by the 8th Michigan.** (jm)

**Col. Daniel Leasure commanded the 100th Pennsylvania Infantry.** (pb/ USAMH)

Behind Fenton's brigade in the assault followed the second brigade commanded by Col. Daniel Leasure, leading his own 100th Pennsylvania (Roundheads), the 79th New York (Highlanders), and the 46th New York, the German "Fremont Regiment." Leasure, a medical doctor by profession, served in the infantry throughout the war.

He put the Highlanders rather than his own regiment in front because many of his men were detailed around the area on other duties, leaving the Roundheads nowhere near full strength. One of the companies, serving as artillery, manned the guns at Battery Stevens and had to wait for its relief, Capt. Charles Strahan's Company I, 3rd Rhode Island Heavy Artillery. Strahan's men later contributed fire support to the Union troops during the fighting. Other Roundhead detachments waited on picket duty and fell in as they could, though only 421 of them managed to return in time to participate in the battle. The Fremonts of the 46th were the third regiment in line.

General Stevens's division moved out around 4:00 a.m. Bringing up the rear trailed Company H, 1st Massachusetts Cavalry under Capt. Lucius M. Sargent, who first detailed four men to stay near Colonel Fenton and carry messages for him as required.

Brigadier General Wright's division, another 3200 men, moved from its camps around Grimball's toward the left of the Federal advance to be able either to hasten to Stevens's aid directly if he needed it or to prevent the Confederates from attacking his left flank. The idea was sound, but problems would arise because of the failure of the Union patrols in previous days to get a clear picture of the topography of the Secessionville peninsula. The Yanks simply did not understand how drastically it narrowed or how nearly impenetrable marshes thoroughly protected both of its flanks. Quite a few Union soldiers soon would pay for this lack of knowledge with their lives.

\*    \*    \*

The leading Union troops from the 8th Michigan approached the Rivers house, just beyond where the Battery Island Road turned north before they were spotted. The house itself stood roughly three-quarters of a mile from the Tower Battery. There is some question as to which Confederate unit provided

the pickets at that point, though they seem to have been from the 9th South Carolina (Pee Dee) Battalion. In any case, having recognized the threat, the Confederates opened fire and wounded five Michigan men from Company H before being overrun.

Looking toward Tower Battery approximately one-half mile away, this road roughly follows the trace of the path along the southern side of the Secessionville Peninsula. The 8th Michigan followed the path in its early morning advance toward the battery. (jm)

The 8th Michigan, numbering 524 officers and men, passed the Rivers house, turned north on the road, then bore off to the right, and advanced a short distance to the first ditch, which covered their entire front. The ditch and parallel hedge marked the edge of the fallow cotton fields, which themselves marked the beginning of the Secessionville peninsula. At that point, the Yanks were more than half a mile from their target. The second ditch, about halfway to the battery from the first, also was lined with a hedge.

Colonel Fenton's forlorn hope began to move forward while the remainder of the regiment moved beyond the hedge and deployed into line for the assault. Somehow, their movements, including the shots fired by the Rivers house pickets, had not yet alerted the Confederate sentinels closer to the Tower Battery. One reasonably may assume that those men, though they probably had heard the firing, simply discounted it as the sort of nervous shooting which sometimes happened on picket lines at night.

One of the Pee Dee pickets apparently avoided capture and rode to warn Col. C. H. Stevens, who commanded the 24th South Carolina and, on that morning, the picket forces of the Advance Guard. Stevens reported hearing the fighting at Secessionville, and shortly thereafter, being told by the rider of the Union attack. He notified Col. Hagood, who later wrote in his *Memoirs* that he immediately sent word

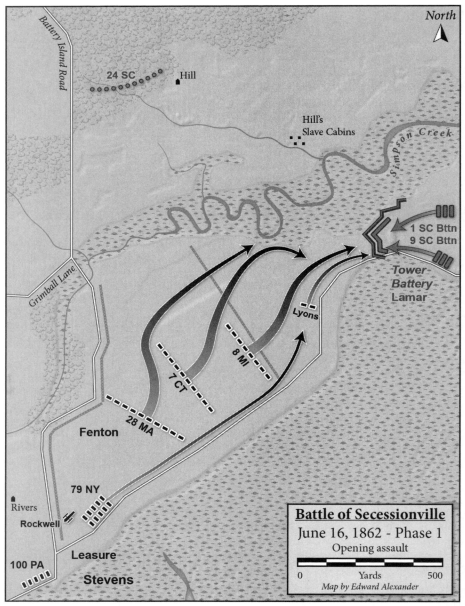

BATTLE OF SECESSIONVILLE—Initial attack by the 8th Michigan followed by other troops of Colonel Fenton's Brigade, General Stevens' Division, beginning about 4:30 a.m. It also shows the arrival of South Carolina troops who first halted the Union advance.

to Col. John McEnery to have the 4th Louisiana Battalion cross to Secessionville on Hatch's Bridge and reinforce Col. Lamar.

Interestingly, Brig. Gen. Evans later claimed in his report that he ordered Col. McEnery forward after meeting with Hagood at the Clark house. It seems more likely that he arrived at Clark's a little too late to have done that. He also claimed to have "commanded in person" during the battle, implying that he had been at or near the Tower Battery. In fact, he never got far from the Clark house.

Yet another problem with Evans's account is his claim that he received word of the attack from Col. Lamar at 2:00 a.m. (two hours before the Union troops stepped off), that he "repaired to Clarke's house as soon as possible," and arrived there at 4:15. It was only about four miles from his headquarters at the Lawton House (to which he had moved from the Royall House the day before) to the Clark House, and most of that route ran on a main road. It is next to impossible to believe that it took more than two hours for him to travel that distance, especially if he knew an attack was underway.

In addition to all of this, Brig. Gen. Evans claimed that he had known on the afternoon of June 15 that an attack was coming either that day or the following morning because Col. Lamar had warned him. Aside from there being no confirmation of this from Lamar himself, it does not ring true because had Evans known, he would have sent substantial reinforcements to the battery well before he did. Moreover, Lamar would hardly have let his men sleep away from their weapons if he had believed an attack was imminent.

Evans had claimed once before in the aftermath of a fight to have known more than he did or even more than he could have. He made a similar claim in his Ball's Bluff report the previous October. Shanks Evans, though hardly alone among Civil War commanders in this regard, was not above padding his resume. His claims about Secessionville, however, seem especially exaggerated.

*    *    *

About 4:30, with dawn just breaking and a drizzling rain falling, the two advanced Michigan companies opened the ball. Still several hundred yards from the battery, they quickened their pace. At some point closer in, they gave a loud cheer and charged, the main body of the regiment being only 40 feet behind them. Colonel Lamar said that when he first saw them, "the enemy were within 700 yards, in line of battle, and advancing on me at the double quick."

Warned by incoming pickets that the Yankees were hot on their heels, Lamar sent a rider to Colonels Gaillard and Smith, commanding the Charleston and Pee Dee Battalions, respectively, with instructions to move their troops up as quickly as possible. Both units were camped at Secessionville, about a half-mile behind the battery. The rider then continued on to notify General Evans at his headquarters near Fort Johnson.

Lieutenant Colonel Peter C. Gaillard had graduated 29th of 56 in the West Point class of 1835 and was a classmate of George Meade. He served as mayor of Charleston just after the war. Lieutenant Colonel Alexander D. Smith, only 23 years old at the time of Secessionville, commanded the unit until he received a severe wound at the Crater in 1864 and was invalided out of the army. He died of tuberculosis in 1867.

After sending messages to these men for help, Lamar ran to the forward wall of the battery and "ordered the 8-inch columbiad to be loaded with grape." Interestingly, this implied that the piece either was unloaded, which seems unlikely, or was loaded with a longer-range round. Perhaps in the excitement of the moment, Lamar simply ordered that the grapeshot be loaded on top of the existing load. In any case, the crew loaded the gun, at which point Lamar aimed it himself and fired directly at the center of the Union line. Just before he did so, Sgt. James Baggott fired the rifled 24-pounder to his left. According to one newspaper report, when Sergeant Baggott fired that first shot, the Union "column was within thirty paces of the guns." Happily for Lamar, Capt. Jamison's detachment arrived just about this time.

Lamar turned the Columbiad over to Lt. Joseph B. Humbert and ordered him to "give them canister freely, which he did." He then sent another messenger to hurry the infantry up to his assistance.

Those first two shots alerted any men not already awake, and the troops rushed either to man the other guns or to grab their muskets. They also devastated the center of the advancing Michigan line. The fight was on.

\*   \*   \*

When Col. Hagood ordered Col. McEnery's 250 Louisianians to cross the bridge and move to aid the men in the battery, he also ordered portions of the 1st and 25th South Carolina (Eutaw Battalion) to move south on the Battery Island Road (portion called Secessionville Road today) and attack the Union flank. They advanced as far as the earthworks and abatis, which they had prepared in the aftermath of the June 10 fighting. This placed them less than 500 yards from where Col. Williams's men of the 3rd New Hampshire and the 3rd Rhode Island Heavy Artillery (serving as infantry), advancing east from Grimball's, would appear as they attempted to get around the flank of the Tower Battery and attack it from that side.

\*   \*   \*

Forced to both flanks by the first destructive fire at the center of their line, the Michiganders tried to regroup. The "forlorn hope" companies moved to their right and luckily discovered a narrow path leading around the southern side of the battery. Quickly taking advantage of this natural cover, they scrambled up the walls and surprised the Confederate gunners by their sudden appearance on the flank. Sergeant Baggott and Captain Reed both were killed almost immediately. Other cannoneers fell dead along with men from the 22nd South Carolina's newly arrived fatigue party, and the fire from that side of the battery halted. Firing down the flank and even into the rear of the Confederate artillery line, the Federals poured it on and nearly won the battle then and there.

Amazingly, fewer than five minutes had passed since Sergeant Baggott had fired the first gun, yet the Michiganders had gotten inside the walls, flanked the Confederate artillery line, and with musketry and their bayonets, delivered what Col. Lamar called a "murderous" attack. At that point, the "forlorn hope" must not have seemed quite so forlorn. A few men from other companies of their regiment joined those already in the fort, and while scattered and not very numerous, at that moment, they were winning. But it was not to last.

In the realm of truth being stranger than fiction, a genuine Hollywood moment is when the cavalry arrives in the nick of time to save the wagon train from the Indians, some 125 men of the 9th South Carolina

**Nothing remains of the Rivers plantation buildings. This spot marks the beginning of the Secessionville peninsula.** (jm)

(Pee Dee) Battalion arrived just as it looked as if the battery would fall. Quickly deploying, they volleyed into the suddenly outnumbered Union troops on their left, then charged and pushed the attackers from inside the battery back across the parapet of the wall, though not away from it. The Yanks simply hunkered down on the outer face of the wall and exchanged fire with the South Carolinians, almost at arms-length across the parapet. As Patrick Brennan wrote, this vicious, close-up fighting over the top of the battery wall "would presage the fighting at Spotsylvania two years later."

The Federals had come very close, but this proved to be the high point of their attack, despite considerable fighting still ahead. Effective Confederate artillery fire combined with the deep, slick pluff mud through which the Union troops had to maneuver delayed timely support and made failure much more likely. Nonetheless, what Brig. Gen. Stevens had called that "bare possibility of success" still existed. Coming up behind the 8th Michigan were the 7th Connecticut, the 28th Massachusetts, and the battery of Connecticut cannoneers.

\*    \*    \*

The Pee Dees, despite their success, faced a developing problem of their own. Their muskets began to malfunction. This was not unusual early in the war when so many obsolete or defective weapons had been hastily acquired and distributed with little or no quality control. Whatever the specific problems, in this case, some of the Confederates suddenly found themselves disarmed in the middle of the fight.

Once the Federals had been pushed back and there was a brief lull, Col. Smith rolled himself over the front of the parapet and collected as many Yankee muskets and cartridge boxes as he could. Loaded down with weapons and gear, he climbed back into the battery and handed them out.

\*    \*    \*

The 8th Michigan companies, which had been forced to the left, managed to form a rough line perhaps ten yards from the base of the wall. The Yanks, who could get close enough enjoyed, relative safety since the Confederates were unable to depress their guns beyond a certain point and the rebel riflemen had to lean over the parapet and expose more of their own bodies in order to fire at them. The Federal fire effectively eliminated the crew of an 18-pounder under Lt. John Bellinger, reducing it to Bellinger himself and two privates, one of whom was his brother. After largely silencing the Confederate artillery, the Michiganders moved forward and nearly reached a position to successfully storm that side of the battery while the rest of the 8th battled with the Pee Dees over the parapet on the other side.

At this point, another Hollywood moment occurred, the second in less than fifteen minutes, when Col. Gaillard and just over 100 men of the 1st South Carolina Infantry (Charleston Battalion) arrived in the wake of the Pee Dee Battalion. The rest of the battalion was with the Advance Guard pickets under Col. Hagood. Later referred to by Hazard Stevens as "the crack corps of the city," the Charleston Battalion, or rather that portion of it, arrived just in time to stop the second part of the 8th Michigan's attack.

Gaillard's troops double-timed into the battery. With Company E, the Calhoun Guard, in the van, they mounted the parapet wall, filled the available spaces between the guns, and contributed their musketry to the defense of the position. The Irish Volunteers, Company C under Capt. William H. Ryan (the same troops who had captured some 20 Union prisoners during the Legare farm fighting on June 3) filed to the left of the battery as directed by Lt. Col. Thomas Wagner of Lamar's artillery battalion. These men became cannoneers as they put their muskets aside and manned the guns which had gone silent under the initial Union onslaught.

Not long after the men of the Charleston Battalion had settled into their work, "Col. Lamar fell from the effect of a Minie ball striking him through the lower part of the ear and running round his neck under the skin." He turned command over to Colonel Gaillard though he remained on the scene, assisting as he could. Gaillard himself later was wounded and passed the command to Wagner.

*   *   *

Initially lagging behind when the 8th Michigan advanced quickly to the assault, Lt. Col. Joseph Hawley's 600 men of the 7th Connecticut fell into some confusion as they worked their way through the second hedge and across the ditch. Colonel Hawley finally managed to untangle the men from the Nutmeg State and get them into a regimental line. Once that was accomplished, and following his orders from Col. Fenton, Hawley obliqued his men to their left in order "to watch and guard against any movement of the enemy on (the 8th Michigan's) left." This order itself revealed the Federal lack of knowledge of the fighting ground. Because of the marsh, the Confederates could not attack from the left, as the men of Col. Williams's brigade soon learned.

Two of the Connecticut guns deployed at the first hedge and contributed their fire to the effort when they could without endangering the other Union soldiers. The cannoneers fired so fast that the gun barrels overheated. Private Thomas Lord burned his hands on one piece as he loaded it and ended up "on his knees cursing like a pirate" from the pain.

The leftward companies of the 7th Connecticut became the first victims of the division's lack of good intelligence about the terrain. With the peninsula narrowing abruptly in front of them, nearly half of the men, pushing through some bushes, suddenly found themselves knee deep in the mud. The resulting confusion disoriented the entire line. The men on the left were the lucky ones, however, as Confederate artillery hit the rightward companies just at that moment and brought any forward movement to a literal dead stop. Colonel Hawley estimated that he was 120 yards from the battery wall. Less than 30 minutes had passed since the beginning of the assault.

Hawley then shifted his men rightward and somewhat to the rear to get them out of the mud so they could regroup. Some of his men, using the trees lining the marsh as cover, started sharpshooting accurately enough to cause the cannonade to briefly slacken, thus buying their comrades the few minutes necessary to move. As the regiment reformed, however, the 520 Irishmen of the 28th Massachusetts came up from behind. Portions of the two units got mixed up, which threw both into further disorder. The Irishmen usually get blamed for this, but Lt. Col. MacLelland Moore faulted the 7th Connecticut, saying that it "fell back and broke through our regiment." Either way, the 28th held in place while the 7th continued to move rightward and gradually disentangle itself. Just after this, Colonel Moore ordered his regiment to withdraw.

This view looks out from Confederate left inside Tower Battery. (jm)

In the midst of this, one Connecticut soldier was killed by a "junk bottle," which had embedded itself in his body. Running low on proper ammunition, the Confederates fired whatever would fit into their cannon, including "chains, glass bottles, scrap iron, (and) horseshoes." One New Yorker picked up a piece of a hammer from the ground and said, "They're firing a whole blacksmith shop at us! Here's the hammer. The anvil will come next." Others mentioned chains, nails, glass, and "every conceivable kind of missile" being fired at them.

About a dozen of the Irishmen, perhaps not hearing Col. Moore's order, pressed forward and joined the men of the 8th Michigan, firing at the

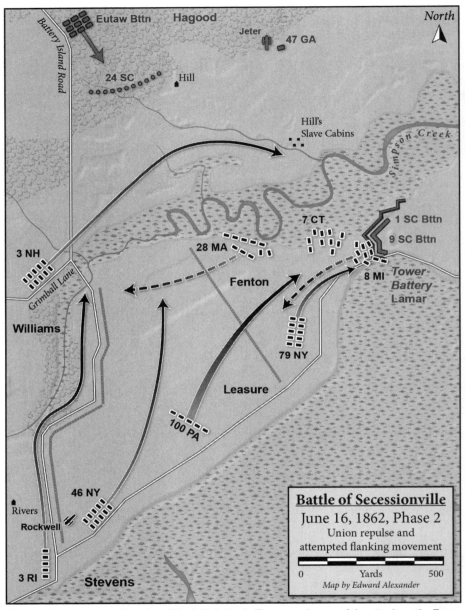

BATTLE OF SECESSIONVILLE—Repulse of the initial attack. The second wave of the attack on the Tower Battery consisting of troops of Colonel Leasure's brigade. It also shows the attempted flanking movement by Union troops north of Simpson's Creek and the marsh, as well as the arrival of the Georgia and South Carolina troops, who countered that attempt.

Confederates atop the parapet. Most either huddled where they were or fell back in disarray as far as the hedge.

Colonel Hawley finally got his men clear and moving across the peninsula to their right, coming up behind the 8th Michigan. He worried about passing directly in front of that fearsome artillery, but the Michigan men had effectively silenced enough of its fire that the 7th made it almost without interference. Unfortunately, the interference they did encounter came from the 79th New York.

The Highlanders were coming up fast as the second wave of the attack began. They passed through the remnants of the Massachusetts formation, stepping on some men and pushing others out of the way. Of those men from the 28th who had gotten back to the hedge, some turned and began to fire again, but they fired erratically and hit at least two of the Michiganders on the Federal left.

This was not the finest hour for the 28th Massachusetts. Although it later would be recognized as a fine fighting unit, its performance at Secessionville did nothing for a reputation that already was shaky from the June 3 skirmish.

With the 28th effectively *hors de combat* and the 7th Connecticut moving rightward across the front of the Tower Battery, the men of the 8th Michigan, occupying both flanks, knew that the assault had failed. They finally began pulling back, though the 7th Connecticut formed behind them, and the 79th New York waited not far away.

General Stevens's second brigade hurried forward with the Highlanders in the lead. It was just after 5:00 a.m., and the fight was far from over.

The Highlanders advanced, but like the 28th Massachusetts on the other side of the peninsula, some of them got entangled with the Connecticut men, slowing the movements of both regiments. Despite the confusion, the New Yorkers pushed through. Once they had done so, the beleaguered Col. Hawley resumed his efforts to get his men into a functional battle line once again.

\*   \*   \*

When Col. Clement Stevens, commanding the 24th South Carolina, heard the firing coming from Secessionville, he was out inspecting his pickets. He immediately ordered Companies D, G, I, and

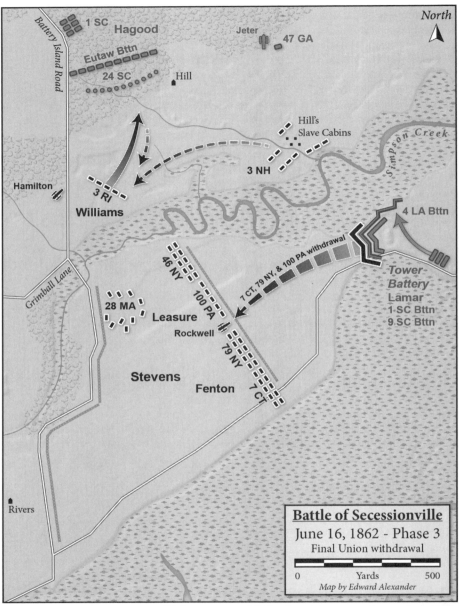

**Battle of Secessionville**

June 16, 1862 - Phase 3

Final Union withdrawal

0                    Yards                    500

*Map by Edward Alexander*

BATTLE OF SECESSIONVILLE—Retreat of Union troops and their attempt to regroup for another attack. This also shows confused fighting north of the Secessionville peninsula and the ultimate withdrawal of the Federals.

K—barely a hundred men in all—to deploy at the previously prepared abatis on the Battery Island Road in the vicinity of today's Bur Clare subdivision. Colonel Hagood joined him there with part of the Charleston Battalion and the 220 men of Lt. Col. Charles Simonton's Eutaw Battalion. Simonton, an attorney and legislator before the war, served as a U.S. circuit court judge later in life.

The Eutaws lined up behind the 24th while the 1st covered the right flank and served as a reserve. This position sat roughly one-half mile north of the Secessionville peninsula. On the left of the line was a field piece under Lt. Berry A. Jeter supported by a company of the 47th Georgia. Before long, these men engaged the New Englanders from Colonel Williams's brigade. As Stevens deployed his men, the Yankees moved up on their left, intending to flank the Tower Battery. Once again, the northerners' lack of terrain knowledge proved problematic.

\*    \*    \*

Advancing through the remnants of the 28th Massachusetts and 7th Connecticut, the men of the 79th New York prepared to face the same artillery which had cut up those regiments so badly. A salvo from the Confederates split the New Yorkers, driving them to the flanks, just as it had done to the Michigan men earlier. Unseen Confederate riflemen in a house by the tower, as well as the South Carolina infantrymen in the fort itself, thinned their ranks even more. Those on the left sought cover by "dropping amongst the cotton ridges in front of the fort." These shallow diggings, perhaps 18 inches deep, paralleled the face of the wall; the men lay lengthwise in them and tried to fire from that awkward position. Lieutenant Colonel David Morrison moved up and down the line on the right instructing his officers, then ordered a charge. Just as the Michiganders had done, the men of the 79th surged over the wall and engaged the desperate remnants of the 9th and 22nd South Carolina in a swirling, fanatical, hand-to-hand brawl. It ended for them as it had for their western comrades. Concentrated Confederate fire overwhelmed them. The New Yorkers fell back, bringing a few stray Michigan men with them.

**Lt. Col. David Morrison led the charge of the 79th New York on the Tower Battery.** (nypl)

This view looks to the west and Grimball's farm. Wright's men approached along this road and bore right as they engaged north of the Secessionville peninsula. (jm)

As they retreated, they heard firing farther out on their left flank. Colonel Williams's twin Thirds, the Third New Hampshire and Third Rhode Island Heavy Artillery, had entered the fray.

Of more immediate interest to the Highlanders just then, however, were the Roundheads who came up after them. Trying to cover the New Yorkers' left, the Pennsylvanians ran into that awful Confederate artillery fire. Company C was "practically atomized," as one historian put it. Only a few men on the right actually made it to the wall. Farther behind them and to the left, the Fremonts followed under Col. Rudolf Rosa, making it only as far as the second hedge where the 28th Massachusetts had tried to regroup. The Irishmen's panic affected the Germans, and several companies simply fled to the rear.

Barely 45 minutes after it had begun, the fighting around the Tower Battery effectively ended when Brig. Gen. Stevens ordered a withdrawal. Captain Rockwell's well-handled 12-pounder field howitzers covered the retreat for the Federal foot soldiers and continued to pound the walls of the battery, helping keep the Confederates' heads down. The various regiments remained in the vicinity of the Battery Island Road, many men hoping to have another go at it and all wondering where General Wright was.

\*    \*    \*

The men in the Tower Battery watched admiringly as the battered Federals on the (Confederate) left front, unlike those on their right front, retreated like soldiers. One reporter wrote that, despite being "under a heavy fire of grape and shell from our battery, the enemy retired in perfect order, closing up the gaps caused by our fire, as if on parade." Perhaps as a tribute to a gallant foe or maybe just taking advantage of an opportunity to catch their breaths and watch the spectacle, the Confederate infantrymen held their fire.

On their right flank, however, at not much farther than musket range, Round Two was about to begin.

*   *   *

Colonel Robert Williams commanded a separate brigade, consisting mostly of artillery, cavalry, and engineer detachments though he also had the 3rd New Hampshire Infantry and five companies of the 3rd Rhode Island Heavies.

The Virginia-born Williams was an 1851 West Point graduate (19th out of 42) and classmate of President Lincoln's brother-in-law, Confederate Brig. Gen. Benjamin Hardin Helm. Williams spent most of the war in the Adjutant General's Office in Washington, eventually becoming Adjutant General of the U.S. Army. In 1866, he married Adele Cutts Douglas, the widow of Senator Stephen A. Douglas.

His brigade usually was associated with, if not directly attached to, General Wright's division. However, as the initial Federal assaults lost steam, Brig. Gen. Stevens asked Brig. Gen. Benham for additional troops. Benham sent Williams.

Major Edwin Metcalf's Companies B, E, F, H, and K of the Rhode Island Heavies led the way, a total of 379 men. Marching east through the woods below the Grimball farm road, they reached the Battery Island Road and saw what was happening to the 79th New York and 100th Pennsylvania in front of the Tower Battery. Some of them ran into the broken fragments of the 28th Massachusetts and stopped to let the Irishmen through.

Colonel John Jackson's Granite State boys moved on the left of the Rhode Islanders and continued marching up "the next finger of land to the north. But they were not quite paralleling the Secessionville peninsula. Instead, as the marsh widened, the Federals angled slightly away from the Confederate position. A few hundred yards past the Battery Island Road, Jackson approached "some shanties that were near the earthworks." These slave cabins stood on the abandoned farm of Washington Hill. Jackson sent Companies A and E forward as skirmishers to secure the cabins, then brought up the rest of his regiment.

Settling there, the colonel must have thought he and his 623 men had hit the jackpot. He was directly on the flank of, even slightly behind, the Tower Battery.

His men were no more than 150 yards away, and the flank walls were low. He wrote, "there was no artillery facing the side I was on and it would have been very easy for me to have gone into the fort." But for the marsh, he would have been right. At that point, few Confederates actually faced him since the Charleston Battalion had suffered heavy casualties, and those still standing focused on the Yankees to their front. Jackson opened fire but soon found that he could not advance. The marsh and creek with the soft, pluff mud bottom effectively blocked his way.

Nonetheless, his regiment's fire was so intense that some of the Rebs thought three full regiments were arrayed on their flank. As the *Mercury* later reported, "The gun carriages were perforated and torn by many balls. Many of our men fell at the guns and along the line formed to the rearward of the battery on its right flank." Some of them tried to turn the Columbiad to face this new threat, but part of the carriage was damaged, so they were unable to do so.

About that time, the Yanks were unpleasantly surprised when fire began coming in from their rear.

\*    \*    \*

The Carolinians under Colonel Stevens sheltered behind the thick abatis and partial earthworks some 200 yards in the rear of Colonel Jackson's men. When Lt. Jeter opened fire with his "brass howitzer," the infantrymen opened fire as well, causing numerous casualties among the Federals. Turning to face this threat, Jackson saw help arriving as the battalion of the 3rd Rhode Island came in from his left rear and positioned itself roughly halfway between his force and the Confederates. These men eventually moved all the way to the abatis, thinking to engage the Rebels at close range and capture the artillery piece. A section from Capt. John Hamilton's Battery E, 3rd U.S. Artillery, also fired on the Confederates from their position back on the Battery Island Road.

About three-quarters of a mile to the northeast, two 24-pounders (probably field howitzers) were arranged as an "enfilade battery near Clark's house." The position later would be named Battery Reed in honor of Capt. Samuel Reed, who died that morning in the Tower Battery. This battery had not yet opened on the Union troops, and Colonel Stevens wanted to know why. He dispatched Lt. Col. Capers to get them into the fight.

**Wright's men continued south down Battery Island (now Secessionville) Road toward the battlefield.** (jm)

When Capers arrived, Lt. John Bunyan Kitching told him that "neither he nor his men knew anything about the guns or the ammunition." Chagrined but undeterred, Capers quickly conducted some basic artillery training for Kitching's men, who either were quick learners or, more likely, despite what Kitching had said, included some among their number with artillery experience.

Capers sighted the pieces himself but neglected to check their placement on the narrow, elevated platforms. The first gun recoiled off the platform when fired and so was out of service for the rest of the battle. The second gun was effectively served throughout.

\*    \*    \*

At that point, Col. Jackson's men saw Confederate reinforcements filing at the double quick into the battery across the marsh. These were the 250 men of Col. McEnery's 4th Louisiana Battalion. Shouting "Remember Butler" as they charged into the battery, they deployed to face the Yanks across the way and soon relieved the pressure on the Tower Battery's gunners. Their improvised battle cry reflected their anger at Union General Benjamin Butler and his infamous "Woman's Order" of May 15, which stated that any woman in Union-held New Orleans who insulted a Union soldier would be "treated as a woman of the town plying her vocation." The Louisiana boys took their anger out on the Yankees across the marsh.

During this 30-minute fight, Sergeant-Major Elbridge Copp of the 3rd New Hampshire witnessed the navy's somewhat erratic fire support, saying that "many of their shells exploded among our own troops" in the fields around the Tower Battery. Several other Union writers also noted the uncomfortable proximity of their own shells. In doing so, they confirmed the fear expressed by Commander Drayton when he informed Commodore Du Pont that he believed "some (of the navy's shells) came much nearer our own men than those of the enemy."

The Hampshiremen faced another problem; they had fired so many rounds that their weapons started fouling badly. Moreover, in the excitement, some of the men neglected to withdraw their rammers when they loaded and so inadvertently fired them into the marsh. Others fired so quickly and carelessly that they came close to hitting the men in the front rank.

Meanwhile, Metcalf's men behind them and the Eutaws with whom they were tangling experienced some confusion of their own. Several of the Rhode Islanders thought the troops to their front were Federals. At the same time, the Eutaws received orders not to fire since part of the 24th South Carolina was in front of them though many of the troops directly to their front were, in fact, the Yankees.

The Rhode Islander's push caused part of the 24th's line to break. Yanks and Rebs mixed together in the dense, tangled maze of fallen trees. Some of the Federals broke through the abatis and reported seeing three artillery pieces ahead. Presumably, one was Jeter's, and the others were the more distant pieces under Colonel Capers. Major Metcalf realized that the 3rd New Hampshire behind him was retiring from the field. Obviously not wanting to be cut off, he ordered his men to withdraw as well, and but for sporadic firing, the fighting ended.

It was about 6:00 a.m.

\*   \*   \*

General Stevens looked at his shattered regiments milling about along the Battery Island Road where they had started and determined to make yet another assault. Over the next 90 minutes, he managed to put a battle line together and move it up to the second hedge in the middle of the field, about 500 yards from the earthwork that those same Yanks had come so very close to taking earlier that morning. From left to right stood the relatively unscathed 46th New York then the badly battered 100th Pennsylvania, 79th New York, and 7th Connecticut with three of the 1st Connecticut Battery's pieces in the center.

Those pieces, together with the big guns of the USS *Pawnee*, engaged in a ferocious artillery duel with the Confederates in the Tower Battery as the regimental commanders awaited what they assumed would be an order to advance.

When ready, Stevens sent Lt. Henry Tafft to find Brig. Gen. Benham on the Battery Island Road somewhere to the north, report that his men were prepared to try again, and to request reinforcements. Tafft did so, but General Benham rebuffed the request. The lieutenant had to return to General Stevens with an order to break off the battle and withdraw his men.

Though angry, Stevens followed the orders. After withdrawing Rockwell's battery one gun at a time, he then ordered the foot soldiers to fall back. In the distance, they all heard the cheers of the Confederates in the battery and across the marsh as those men finally realized that they had won.

After it was all over and the attack had failed, Captain Sargent's 28 horse soldiers, having protected and screened the division's left flank during the fighting and suffered several casualties in the process, fell in behind the retreating infantrymen. The troopers acted as a rear guard in case the Confederates initiated a pursuit from the Tower Battery. The Confederates were in no shape to do that, and Hazard Stevens pithily summed it up. "The enemy attempted no pursuit," he wrote, "and by 10 a.m. the entire force was back in camp."

Confederate Lt. Iredell Jones honestly and soberly wrote, "But while we give all credit to our own troops, let us never again disparage our enemy and call them cowards, for nothing was ever more glorious than their three charges in the face of a raking fire of grape and canister, and then at last, as if to do or die, they broke into two columns and rushed against our right and left flanks, which movement would have gained the day, had not our reinforcements arrived."

With that, it was over. Quiet finally settled onto the fields around Secessionville—broken only by the cries and groans of wounded men.

# *Your Gun Deserves to Be Mounted on a Golden Pivot*

## CHAPTER TWELVE

*AFTER THE BATTLE*

Shortly after the battle, Maj. Gen. Pemberton rewarded Col. Lamar's courage and leadership when he ordered the Tower Battery henceforth to be called Fort Lamar. Lamar did not live to enjoy the honor for long, however, as he was stricken with malaria and died on October 18, 1862.

Captain J. B. Humbert, who commanded the Columbiad in the Tower Battery, did, however, live to enjoy his laurels for many years. As an old man reminiscing about his role, he joyfully recounted the praise of one of his comrades. "After the battle," he wrote, "Capt. F. N. Bonneau came to my battery and said to me, 'Lieutenant, your gun deserves to be mounted on a golden pivot.'"

\* \* \*

Colonel Johnson Hagood called the battle of Secessionville "one of the decisive engagements of the war." When one thinks of what might have happened, that certainly is true.

Asking "what if?" about any battle is an endlessly fascinating exercise. Though pointless in some respects, it nonetheless remains appealing to historians. With Secessionville, at least, we know exactly what some of the participants thought and talked about at the time.

It was a small fight and quickly forgotten since the Seven Days battles around Richmond began less

**Following the battle, the Confederates buried several hundred Union dead in this area about 100 yards in front of the battery. (jm)**

**Alfred Waud made sketches of the Charleston waterfront, James Island, and Fort (Castle) Pinckney, drawn shortly after the Union occupation of Charleston.** (loc)

than two weeks later. But it would not have been so quickly forgotten if the Federals had won. Such a victory almost surely would have led to the fall of Charleston, and that might have changed everything. That, at least, was the view of Brig. Gen. Wilmot De Saussure, Adjutant General and Inspector General of South Carolina. Saussure wrote to General P. G. T. Beauregard less than a month after the battle that "had Secessionville been taken, I believe that the whole eastern line would have fallen in forty-eight hours."

Lieutenant Colonel Ellison Capers agreed. If the Yanks "were to have (taken the battery), their gun boats could run up the creek & shell the redoubts & lines, which would drive us away from this end, & in that way they would have successfully turned our flank."

Lieutenant Iredell Jones wrote, "Secessionville . . . constitutes our extreme left flank, and if taken the enemy could turn our left. It was for this reason, no doubt, that the attack was made."

Had Charleston fallen in June 1862, the Seven Days battles, at least in the form they occurred, might not have happened because the Confederate government would have had to consider the new situation in South Carolina. Would Jefferson Davis have approved General Lee's offensive actions against the Union army around Richmond at that time with supplies from and communication with the Deep South suddenly imperiled?

Other possibilities abound. As Milby Burton has written, "With its deep-water harbor and its railroads

A post-war image from 1865 shows Charleston in the background. Castle Pinckney played only a minor role during the war, briefly serving to house Union prisoners from First Manassas. (loc)

leading into the interior, Charleston would have given the Union armies an excellent staging area." Might a quick inland thrust by the Federals, using the captured city of Charleston as a base, have pulled troops from Virginia to protect supply lines and thus hindered the defense of Richmond? What about Savannah? Wilmington? Atlanta's railroad junction?

Not everyone was so sure, however. Captain Alfred Rockwell wrote, "If we had taken the fort that morning, we would not have been really any nearer Charleston. . . . Their main line back of the fort was much stronger." Rockwell seems to have been in the minority on this, though he did say that the Federals would have taken the fort "if the attacking column had not set up a cheer . . . but had advanced silently" and surprised the sleeping rebs.

In any case, the writer has come to believe that the fall of Charleston in June 1862 would have changed the entire tenor of the war if, but only if, the Federals had followed up their victory by using the city, as Burton noted above. Taking Charleston and just holding it would have accomplished little beyond cutting off another port for the blockade runners. Certainly, northern morale would have skyrocketed while southern morale would have plummeted, but morale, like momentum in a football game, can change quickly. Further successful action by Maj. Gen. Hunter still would have been required.

Regardless of what might have happened, what did happen is clear. Aside from stopping the Union assault, the Confederates made some minor but useful gains in terms of materiel. They captured over 200

Fort Johnson was the key to Charleston Harbor. Had the Federals been able to take it, Charleston itself would have fallen. Fort Sumter is in the distance. (loc)

Springfield and Enfield rifles and muskets and large quantities of ammunition, cartridge boxes, and other gear.

On the other hand, the casualties, though well to Confederate advantage in terms of raw numbers, were proportionally similar. The Union force suffered 683 total casualties, or about 20% of the attacking troops. This broke down to 107 killed, 487 wounded, and 89 captured or missing.

The corresponding Confederate numbers were 52 killed, 144 wounded, and 8 missing, or about 16% of the force involved. As always, the Confederacy could not replace its battlefield losses as easily as the Union could.

\*   \*   \*

What went wrong for the Federals? Clearly, Brig. Gen. Benham deserves the blame for inadequate overall planning and lack of proper reconnaissance.

General Benham accused Brig. Gen. Stevens of not getting his support troops up quickly enough

and, in this, he was at least partly justified. The 7th Connecticut and the units behind it were too far behind to effectively support the temporarily successful assault of the 8th Michigan. Had even one regiment been close enough to the Michiganders, those "Hollywood moments" for the Confederates likely would not have mattered. As the division commander on the ground, Stevens must bear the responsibility for this.

That said, Stevens did attempt to regroup after the initial failure in a way that would have corrected the faults in Benham's original plan. That attempt was thwarted when Benham decided that the battle had been lost, then ordered Stevens to break off the attack and withdraw. Stevens was furious about this, but orders are orders.

Benham also might be censured for his failure to properly coordinate with the navy, something which likely played a larger role in the fighting than usually is credited. Of course, the pluff mud and the well-served Confederate artillery played major roles as well. Taken together, however, the events which made up the overall Federal failure come back to Henry Benham's very poor leadership and abysmally bad planning.

**Note how Confederates disabled the guns at Fort Johnson by chopping out a portion of the carriage. The city of Charleston is in the distance.** (loc)

\*   \*   \*

As for General Benham himself, a thorough look at his personality and generalship is not within the scope of this work. Suffice it to say that Benham was a better engineer than he was an infantry officer.

Did he ignore General Hunter's orders? Hunter felt that he did and, as a result, arrested and relieved him of command and sent him back to Washington. But Benham did not advance on Charleston or on Fort Johnson, the two actions that Hunter specifically had forbidden. What he might have done had the Federals succeeded at Secessionville is open to speculation, but there is nothing in the orders that Benham gave to Stevens and Wright to indicate that the movement was anything but an attack on the Tower Battery, even if Benham did later hedge his bets by calling it a reconnaissance-in-force. Such an attack seems to have been within the scope of General Hunter's instructions.

It is the writer's opinion, therefore, that Brig. Gen. Benham did not violate Maj. Gen. Hunter's orders. However, he did antagonize all his immediate subordinates with whom, especially Brig. Gen. Stevens, he was on bad terms anyway. He pressed the attack before his troops were ready, and he too willingly evaded all responsibility for what happened. In the end, the attack at Secessionville failed. Had it succeeded, events would have developed in a completely different way, regardless of anyone's feelings about Benham's alleged violation of orders.

Perhaps most importantly for historians, whatever Isaac Stevens or anyone else personally thought of Benham, and however justified their feelings may have been, Joseph Holt, the Judge Advocate General of the United States Army, conducted a full investigation of Brig. Gen. Benham's actions at Secessionville and, in January 1863, exonerated him.

However, exoneration did not mean all that Brig. Gen. Benham might have hoped. He lost his volunteer commission as a brigadier general and never again commanded troops in the field. He was reinstated in the army as a lieutenant colonel of engineers and given command of the Engineer Brigade of the Army of the Potomac, where he performed creditably. He ended the war as a brevet brigadier general.

\*   \*   \*

On June 27, Maj. Gen. Hunter ordered the abandonment of James Island. Troops packed their gear and dismantled their camps, transports arrived, and over the next several days, the Union soldiers reversed the routes they had taken from Hilton Head a month earlier. By July 7, they were gone.

However, the men who fought the battle would always remember it. On November 29, 1863, the 79th New York Highlanders manned positions in Fort Sanders near Knoxville, Tennessee, where General James Longstreet's Confederate troops assailed them. Now inside an earthwork rather than storming it themselves, some of the men shouted, over all the din of battle, "Remember James Island! Remember James Island!"

For the Confederates, Secessionville was a small but significant early war victory that must have boosted morale throughout the South and not least with the troops then defending Richmond.

**This view from the Union left shows approximately where the 7th Connecticut found itself suddenly mired in pluff mud and water.** (jm)

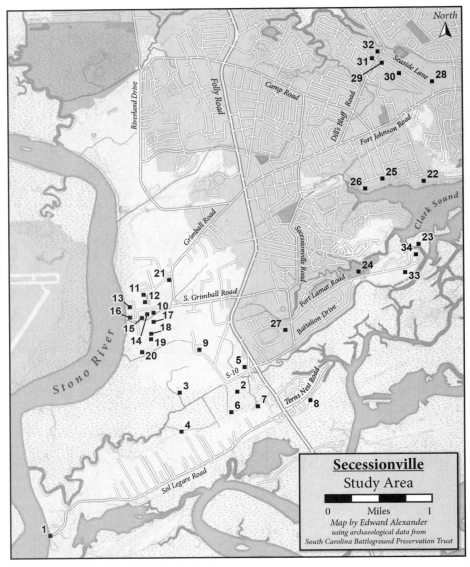

SECESSIONVILLE—Locations of battle-related sites overlaid on a modern map, based on a study area map developed by (and used with permission of) the South Carolina Battleground Preservation Trust.

# Driving Tour of the Battle of Secessionville

## APPENDIX A

The fighting around Secessionville took place on James Island, South Carolina. This driving tour covers that area and can easily be followed using the South Carolina Battlefield Trust's map of the "Study Area" as a guide. That map is printed here with the kind permission of the Trust. It clearly overlays the key battle-related sites onto a modern road map and identifies them by a series of numbers from 1 – 34.

Sadly, you will notice that there is not much in the way of war-era structures to see on this driving tour other than the Tower Battery itself. Life moved on, and so you will be viewing historic locations with little of the period remaining on them.

Most visitors will drive to James Island from Charleston. To do this, take US Route 17 South (Savannah Highway) out of Charleston, cross the Ashley River, then merge left onto SC Route 171 (Folly Road). Note that Folly Road is confusingly—though only for a short stretch—called Folly Road Boulevard before resuming the shorter form of the name.

After less than a mile, Folly Road crosses the Wappoo Creek over a drawbridge. Once across the bridge, you are on James Island. The road then continues south approximately seven miles to Folly Island and Folly Beach. Note that the modern Folly Road did not exist at the time of the war, but many of the roads on either side of it did. They are part of this driving tour.

To begin your tour at the Union landing site on Battery Island, continue south on Folly Road for about six miles. Turn right onto Sol Legare Road and drive 2.5 miles to the landing site on the Stono River. The spot is marked as "1" on the Study Area Map. There is parking on either side of the road at the landing. It was here that Union forces under Brig. Gen. Isaac Stevens landed on the afternoon of June 2, 1862.

The Union forces approached from downriver, or to the left, as you look at the river from the landing site. Farther upriver, to the right, are the sites of Brig. Gen. Horatio Wright's camps and Confederate Fort Pemberton.

**A cemetery now sits on the site of Battery Stevens.** (jm)

Go back on Sol Legare Road about two miles to its intersection with a dirt track called Old Sol Legare Road. Turn left here and go 0.25 miles to spot "6" on the Study Map. That is as far as you will be able to go as you are, in effect, at the end of a long driveway. Spot "6" roughly marks the south end of the access road to the Rivers Causeway but is now private property, and nothing can clearly be seen due to the foliage and houses. Go back to the intersection and park on the side of the road.

You will not be able to get to spot "2," where Captain Chichester lost his three carronades, but you should understand that the June 3 fighting extended south from there, past "6," to the intersection of Sol Legare Road and Old Sol Legare Road where you now are standing. The LeGare house was on the NW corner of the intersection. The outbuildings used as cover by part of the 100th Pennsylvania were across the Sol Legare Road and just to the east. It was around those cabins where 20 of the "Roundheads" were captured during the fight.

While you are here, take note of the monument to the 54th Massachusetts. It was on this site, about a year after the battle of Secessionville, that the 54th first was bloodied in action against Confederate forces.

Just to the west are spots "3" and "4," which mark the access to Grimball's Causeway. This causeway played no role in our story and is, in any case, inaccessible.

From here, return to Folly Road. Go directly across it onto Terns Nest Road. A short distance ahead on the right is the Stem Point Memorial Cemetery. This is spot "8" on the map and was the location of Battery Stevens. Return to Folly Road, turn right, and then left into the parking lot of the Treasure Island store directly across Folly Road from the River Front Community sign. From here, walk north about 75 yards along the west side of Folly Road to the horse gate. There may be considerable traffic in this area, and the shoulder of the road is narrow, so exercise appropriate caution. As you look through the gate down an overgrown roadway, you will see a thick tree line perhaps 200 yards distant. This marks the approximate site of Battery Williams, spot "7" on the map. There is nothing left of either Battery Stevens or Battery Williams. You will only be looking at the respective sites.

**The walking trail at Fort Lamar offers a chance to explore part of the Secessionville battlefield.** (cm)

Return to your car, then continue north on Folly Road. Drive 0.3 miles, then turn left on S-10/Battery Island Drive. Go 0.1 miles, cross Old Folly Road, and continue straight another 0.2 miles to where the road makes a sharp right turn. Stop at the gate on the left. This gate marks the access road to spot "5," the north end of the Rivers Causeway. As at spot "6," you cannot go any farther because it is private property. The causeway crossed the marsh ahead of you between spots "5" and "6."

Drive back to Folly Road. Turn left and drive 0.5 miles to South Grimball Road to see spots 10-21, the area of Brig. Gen. Wright's headquarters and camps around the Grimball Plantation. To get there, turn left on South Grimball Road. Just past the James Island Elementary School on the right, bear left onto the dirt road called Grimball Farm Lane. Follow it to the dead end. Ahead are modern buildings on the site of the Grimball house and outbuildings. Do not go beyond this spot as it is private property.

Turn left and continue along the dirt track. Again, there are modern structures here, but this is the area where Wright's regimental camps and division hospital were located. See the corresponding numbers on the Study Area Map.

Proceed back along the farm lane to South Grimball Road and make a sharp left. After about 1.5 miles, this will bring you back to Folly Road. Continue straight across it. The road changes names here and is called Fort Johnson Road. This is the old King's Highway on historic maps. Just past this intersection on the left is the James Island Presbyterian Church. It is not marked on the Study Area Map, but was the site of the wartime church of the same name where the Confederates maintained a forward observation post. It also was the site of the June 7 skirmish between the 7th Connecticut and 24th South Carolina. Near here is where Union Pvt. Milton Woodford was captured.

**Stem Point Cemetery now occupies the former site of Battery Stevens.** (jm)

Continue 0.5 miles to "Artillery Crossroads," the intersection of Fort Johnson Road and Secessionville Road. Also not marked on the map, this crossroads was about 2 miles southwest of the camps of most of the Confederate units. There is nothing left of the camps, of course, but if you wish to view the sites, proceed about 0.4 miles to Dill's Bluff Road and turn left. After 1 mile, look for Seaside Land and Sigsbee Road on the right. Just past Sigsbee Road, Dill's Bluff Road makes a sharp bend to the left. In this area were the camps marked "29," "31," and "32" on the map. Spots "28" and "30" are a short distance down Seaside Lane.

Continue down Seaside Lane back to Fort Johnson Road and turn left if you wish to see the site of Fort Johnson, located where the road dead-ends about three miles farther on. The site today is a marine biology research facility. All that is left of Fort Johnson is an old brick powder magazine and the poorly preserved remnants of Civil War earthworks. Near the magazine is a monument at the approximate location of the mortar battery from which the opening shot of the war was fired onto Fort Sumter.

If you do not wish to go to Fort Johnson, turn right from Seaside Lane onto Fort Johnson Road and drive back to Artillery Crossroads, where you will then turn left onto Secessionville Road. Drive 1.5 miles to the modern Fort Lamar Road and turn left. Note that Secessionville Road becomes Old Military Road shortly before you arrive at the turn.

Drive about 0.75 miles and turn left into the Fort Lamar Heritage Preserve parking lot. Here you will see two commemorative monuments to the participants and an information kiosk. From here, you also will be able to walk around the well-preserved remnants of the Tower Battery itself.

Having done that, you might turn left out of the parking lot and go about 0.5 miles to the approximate site of the 9th South Carolina's camp at spot 33. Again, however, there is nothing left of the camp. Modern houses are in the area, and the road dead-ends at the entrance to private property. You will not be able to get to spots "23" or "34."

Alternatively, you may turn right out of the kiosk parking lot and go about 100 yards. Turn left onto Battalion Drive, which, where it parallels Secessionville Creek, was the track followed by the Union forces during their assault. This will take you back to Old Military Road just about at spot "27," the site of the

**The 4th Louisiana position looking across the marsh.** (jm)

Rivers house. Turn left and follow the road. You will see that you have made a large loop which has taken you back to Folly Road near where you began.

Turn right onto Folly Road and drive north back toward Charleston. As you approach the drawbridge over Wappoo Creek, look for the stoplight at Tatum Street. Just past this light, bear left onto Old Folly Road, go one block and turn left onto Maybank Highway. Go 1.5 miles and turn right onto Riverland Drive, which will take you to the site of Fort Pemberton.

After 0.2 miles, turn left onto Aubrey Drive. Go one block to the corner of Aubrey and Yates. On the left is the southeast corner of Fort Pemberton. This is not marked on the Study Area Map. It is heavily overgrown and posted as private property, so you will only see parts of the remaining earthwork as you drive or walk around the exterior.

Go back to Riverland Drive, turn left, and proceed 0.5 miles to the dead-end at the confluence of the Stono River and the Wappoo Cut. The cut connects the Stono with the Ashley River and was strategically valuable. Fort Pemberton protected it and served as the northwestern anchor of the Confederate James Island defenses.

From here, turn around, go back the way you came on Riverland Drive, turn left on Maybank, and proceed back to Charleston.

Despite the lack of structures from the time of the war, the battle of Secessionville remains a fascinating study. It is the author's hope that this driving tour and the Study Area Map will help you get a feel for the lay of the land and to gain an appreciation for the battle itself.

Mansion of the Rebel Genl Thomas F Drayton
Hilton Head, S.C.

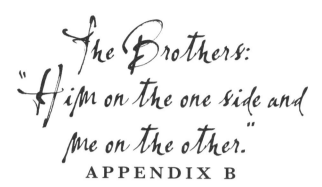

# The Brothers:
## "Him on the one side and me on the other."

### APPENDIX B

Aside from Thomas and Percival Drayton, at least one other pair of brothers fought on opposite sides at Secessionville. Unlike the Draytons, James and Alexander Campbell were both right in the middle of the Secessionville fighting itself, though neither knew it at the time.

The Campbell brothers hailed from Crieff, Scotland, and had come to the United States in the early 1850s. James settled in Charleston, Alexander in New York City.

Alexander, generally known as "Sandy," moved to Charleston in 1856, where he worked as a stone mason and helped to build the United States Custom House on East Bay Street. He even served for a time in a local militia company. For reasons of his own, he decided to move back to New York in 1859. His departure from Charleston seems to have marked the last time he ever saw his older brother, James.

Lieutenant James Campbell fought with the Union Light Infantry, Company F, 1st South Carolina Infantry, a.k.a, the Charleston Battalion. His brother, Sgt. Alexander Campbell was a color bearer in the 79th New York Highlanders. Each of these units had been part of its state's militia organization before the war.

Pure chance brought the brothers near each other in June 1862. The Highlanders were part of Brig. Gen. Isaac Stevens's division and thus part of the James Island landing force.

On the morning of June 16, 1862, the Charleston battalion rushed into the Tower Battery and deployed in time to repel an assault by part of the 8th Michigan on the battery's right. In his haste, James Campbell had left his pistol in camp and arrived on the battlefield without a weapon. This resulted in the colorful and often told story of how he pushed a heavy head log from the parapet down onto several Union soldiers who were scrambling up the exterior slope, knocking them down with the rolling log as if they had been bowling pins. He remained in the thick of the fight throughout the battle.

**The Drayton family home was on Hilton Head.** (loc)

Capt. Percival Drayton on the left, with Adm. David Farragut. Drayton was a South Carolinian who remained in the U.S. Navy and opposed his Confederate brother during the battle for Port Royal. (loc)

Though they never actually met on the field, the Campbell brothers probably were little more than a hundred yards apart at any given time. Alexander advanced with the Highlanders on the other side of the battery later in the fighting. Both survived the battle, and neither was wounded.

Alexander learned in the aftermath of the June 3 skirmish that James was nearby. A captured Confederate soldier who knew his brother commented on the family resemblance and informed Alexander that James was a popular member of the Charleston battalion who had been elected a second lieutenant in his company.

Likewise, James learned from captured Union soldiers after the fight at Secessionville that his brother had been present on the field. On June 18, he sent a letter to Alexander under a flag of truce, expressing the hope that they would "never again meet face to face Bitter enemies in the Battle field." However, he told his brother that, should that happen, "You have but to discharge your deauty to Your caus for I can assure you I will strive to discharge my deauty to my country & My cause."

Alexander wrote to his wife in late June, telling her, "Its rather too bad to think that we should be fighting him on the one side and me on the other." A local paper highlighted this same point a few days later. "The case of Mr. Campbell affords another illustration of the deplorable consequences of this fratricidal war. The color bearer of the 79th Highlanders who fought gallantly in the late action and carried his colors off safely, is a brother of Lieutenant Campbell. They had both been fighting each other hard without recognition."

The brothers had one more chance to meet in peace on July 3. James approached the Union pickets under a flag of truce, asking if he might be allowed to see his brother. The Union officer in charge of the pickets declined to arrange a meeting but did agree to pass along a letter. It was too late for Alexander to do anything about it since the Highlanders left James Island for good on the following morning.

Alexander left the army in May 1863 and returned to New York City. James was captured in the fighting at Battery Wagner in July 1863 and spent the remainder of the war as a POW. The brothers corresponded during that time but apparently did not see each other.

After the war, James farmed in the Charleston area until his death in 1907. Alexander worked as a stone mason in Middletown, Connecticut, until his own death in 1909.

(Note that the information in this appendix is taken from the article by J. Tracy Power and the book by Terry A. Johnston. See the online bibliography.)

**Drayton commanded Confederate forces at Port Royal and opposed his brother, Union naval Captain Percival Drayton, in that fight. He also was president of the Charleston and Savannah Railroad.** (du)

# *Order of Battle*

## THE BATTLE OF SECESSIONVILLE

### JAMES ISLAND, SC
### June 16, 1862

### CONFEDERATE ORDER OF BATTLE
Field Commander of Troops Engaged
Brig. Gen. Nathan G. Evans

**Tower Battery**: Col. Thomas G. Lamar
Companies B and I, 1st South Carolina Artillery • 22nd South Carolina (detachment) • 9th South Carolina (Pee Dee) Battalion • 1st South Carolina (Charleston) Battalion, 6 companies • 4th Louisiana Battalion

**Advanced Forces**: Col. Johnson Hagood
1st South Carolina • 25th South Carolina (Eutaw) Battalion • 24th South Carolina (detachment) • Boyce's (Jeter's) Light Battery (one gun) • Clarks Point Battery (later Battery Reed; 2 guns) • 1st South Carolina Artillery (detachment)

**Other Troops**
47th Georgia • 51st Georgia

### UNION ORDER OF BATTLE
Field Commander of Troops Engaged
Brig. Gen. Henry Benham

**First Division**: Brig. Gen. Horatio Wright
First Brigade: Col. J. L. Chatfield
6th Connecticut • 47th New York • 97th Pennsylvania

**Second Brigade**: Col. Thomas Welsh
45th Pennsylvania • 76th Pennsylvania • Battery E, 3rd U.S. Art'y

**Second Division**: Brig. Gen. Isaac I. Stevens
First Brigade, Col. William M. Fenton
8th Michigan • 28th Massachusetts • 7th Connecticut

**Second Brigade**: Col. Daniel Leasure
79th new York • 100th Pennsylvania • 46th New York

**Third Brigade**: Col. Robert Williams
3rd New Hampshire • 3rd Rhode Island Heavy Artillery (acting as infantry) • 1st Massachusetts Cavalry • 1st New York Engineers • 1st Connecticut Battery

# *Suggested Reading*

## THE BATTLE OF SECESSIONVILLE

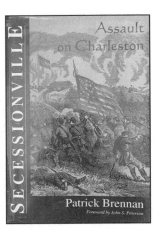

*Secessionville: Assault on Charleston*
Patrick Brennan
Savas Publishing Co., 1996
ISBN: 1-882810-08-2

This was the first full-length tactical work on the battle and has set a high bar for subsequent studies.

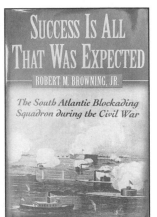

*Success Is All That Was Expected: The South Atlantic Blockading Squadron During the Civil War*
Robert M. Browning, Jr.
Brassey's, Inc., 2002
ISBN: 1-57488-514-6

Though covering much more than naval activities around Charleston, this superb recounting of the Union blockade helps the reader to understand the vital role played by the navy in the short Secessionville campaign.

*The Siege of Charleston, 1861-1865*
E. Milby Burton
University of South Carolina, 1970
ISBN: 0-87249-345-8

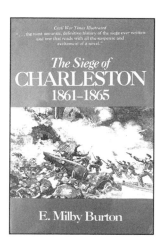

Burton provides a good summary of the
Secessionville fighting within the larger context of
the war in and around Charleston.

*Charleston Blockade: The Journals of John B. Marchand,
US Navy, 1861-62*
Craig L. Symonds, editor
Naval War College Press, 1976
ASIN: B00010Q9EA

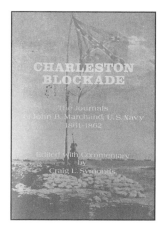

Marchand's journal of his time as commander
of the Charleston blockading force includes a
great deal of information on the Secessionville
campaign.

# About the Author

**Jim Morgan** is a co-founder and past president of the Fort Sumter Civil War Round Table in Charleston, SC. He is a member of the board of the Fort Sumter-Fort Moultrie Historical Trust. He also is a past president of the Loudoun County Civil War Roundtable in Leesburg, VA, and was a co-founder and chairman of the Friends of Ball's Bluff. His previous work includes a tactical study of Ball's Bluff titled *A Little Short of Boats: The Battles of Ball's Bluff and Edwards Ferry* and a chapter on the Joint Committee on the Conduct of the War for ECW's Turning Points of the Civil War. He also has written for *Civil War Times*, *America's Civil War*, *The Artilleryman*, *Blue & Gray*, and other periodicals. Retired in 2014 from the State Department, Jim spends much of his time as a National Park Service volunteer at Forts Sumter and Moultrie.